PAWNONOMICS

A Tale of the Historical, Cultural, and Economic
Significance of the Pawnbroking Industry

Steve Krupnik

Published in USA by Cloud Ten Inc
808 Trailridge East
Mishawaka, IN 46544
Visit www.pawnonomics.com for further updates on the pawnbroking industry

ISBN: 1-4392-2573-7
LCCN: 2009900575
EAN13: 9781439225738

Visit www.booksurge.com to order additional copies.

Pop Goes the Weasel

Half a pound of tuppenny rice,
Half a pound of treacle.
That's the way the money goes,
Pop! goes the weasel.
Up and down the City road,
In and out the Eagle,
That's the way the money goes,
Pop! goes the weasel.

To "pop" is the slang word for "pawn." Weasel is derived from "weasel and stoat" meaning coat. It was traditional for even poor people to own a suit, which they wore as their "Sunday Best." When times were hard they would pawn their suit, or coat, on a Monday and claim it back before Sunday.

"A Birmingham Backstreet Boyhood shows how tough times were;
you hoped nobody noticed you going to the 'pop shop' to pawn precious
valuables to get enough money to pay the rent or buy food for the family."
A Birmingham Backstreet Boyhood
by Graham Twist

The head cashier of the local branch of Noreast Bank, a Miss Patricia Wax (known to her friends as Patty), was surprised one day to see a small green frog walk up to her counter.

"Good morning" said the frog "I'd like to take out a loan of £30,000, please."

"One moment, sir" said Patty "Can I have your name please?"

"Certainly" said the frog "I'm Kermit Jagger, son of Mick Jagger."

"Oh yes!" said Patty, in a slightly concerned manner "And what will you be putting up as collateral against the loan?"

"I'll leave this small, china statue of the leaning tower of Pisa"

"Please wait one moment, sir" said Patty "I'll need to check this with the manager."

With that said, she went off to see the manager, Mr. Martin, to obtain his views on the proposed loan.

"Mr. Martin, sir." she said "There's a small green frog outside who claims to be a son of Mick Jagger and is asking for a loan of £30,000 with this china ornament as collateral. What do you think?"

The manager was furious at her incompetence and shouted in a very abrupt manner, "It's a knick knack, Patty Wax, give the frog a loan. His old man's a Rolling Stone!"

The Institution of Silly & Meaningless Sayings (ISMS)
http://www.isms.org.uk/proverbials.htm

This book is dedicated to the memory of Miley O'Neal and Charles R Jones. The two most forward thinking pawnbrokers I've had the privilege to know.

CONTENTS

INTRODUCTION

A VENERABLE INSTITUTION OR A DEN OF THIEVES?

Pawnbrokers have been portrayed, for the most part, as stingy usurers, a shade above loan sharks. Is this a justified portrayal? Certainly there are thieving pawnbrokers, just like there are thieves on Wall Street. But while history can perceive a man like John D. Rockefeller as both a "robber baron" who made his millions by unethical and illegal means, and an "industrial statesman" whose actions should not be judged morally, pawnbrokers are not given this same analytical treatment.

Although commonly understood to mean charging "excessive interest," the Oxford English Dictionary defines usury as "the fact or practice of lending money at interest." Clearly, then, all respectable lending institutions (banks, credit cards, mortgage brokers, etc.) engage in usury.

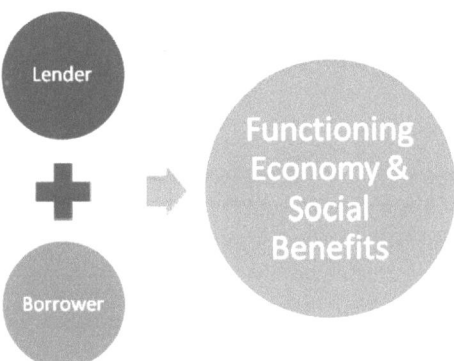

Usury can be not only a mutually beneficial arrangement, but it can also be a vital factor in the health and growth of an economy. Without access to funds, many of our greatest achievements as individuals, families, companies, and even countries could not have occurred. And in fact, one of the most famous stories in historic achievement—Christopher Columbus's discovery of America—was only possible because Queen Isabella was ready to pawn her crown jewels to fund the trip.

So what explains the negative perception of pawnbrokers? In large part this has to do with issues of class perception. After all, Wall Street and the modern day "robber barons" who ran empires like Lehman Brothers, Enron, and AIG hobnob with presidents and senators. The wealthy class protects and insulates itself, with a wealthy media funded by advertising dollars of wealthy companies, much better than the working-class financial and business institutions. Even the anti-Semitism that arose because of biblical passages that allowed Jews to openly lend money to Christians in societies where Jews were shut out of other trades[1] was tied to class status. Catholic Church officials ignored the lending practices (usury) of the Florentine *bankers* of the Medici family even while condemning Jewish or non-Catholic non-merchant class *pawnbrokers*.[2]

The other common philosophical arguments are that money in and of itself does not "produce" anything (Aristotle was the forefather of this line of thinking) and that the lender does not share the risk and labor equally with the borrower. The Federal Reserve, a private U.S. entity, is able to lend money that it is literally allowed to print as legal American tender at the cost of the taxpaying citizen, and then charge interest that never comes back to the citizenry. The idea that money isn't productive is understood to be false in an industrialized society. The sharing of risk argument, especially after the enormous bailout U.S. taxpayers are being forced to pay for while receiving very little of the rewards, is worth exploring in more depth, and this book will do that. The irony is that in reality a pawnbroker has always offered a much fairer business transaction than most "traditional" and more respected lenders, including banks.

Lastly, the attitude toward usury by Jews, Christians, and Muslims was historically condemned primarily on biblical/moral grounds. In addition to the fact that the Bible explicitly forbids it (except if with one's enmies or outsiders),[3]

---

1.   Walter Laqueur, *The Changing Face of Anti-Semitism: From Ancient Times to the Present Day* (New York: Oxford University Press, 2006).

2.   Cardinal Hostiensis in 1260 specifically allows for a merchant's claim of compensation (interest) for the opportunity cost—"lucrum cessans," John T. Noonan Jr., *The Scholastic Analysis of Usury* (Cambridge: Harvard University Press, 1957).

3.   Hebrew Bible, 1917 Jewish Publication Society translation, Deuteronomy, 23:20–21.

profit made by lending money (interest) was considered unearned and exploit-ative. Medieval scholars even argued that since interest was only earned by the input of time itself, the lender was attempting to steal time, which was per-ceived as owned by God.[4] Even worse, since pawnbrokers were often the only ones who would lend to the poor, they were seen as profiting by exploiting the "meek" and regarded as evil "self-interest." We will place the concept behind this rhetorical moral framework historically and through the present day and show that in reality this paternalistic, condescending morality is far more exploitative and damaging than the productive, enlightened self-interest of a fair business arrangement.

This book will not only relate some of the fascinating history of pawnbrokering (as collateral lending) and entertain you with some sardonic comparisons to those more "respectable" institutions of modern finance, but it will also dispel some common myths and misperceptions. You may or may not come away with an enlightened perspective, but it will certainly be entertaining and probably conversational.

---

4. R. H. Tawney, "Historical Introduction" to *A Discourse Upon Usury*, by,Dr Thomas Wilson (London, 1925).

CHAPTER ONE

WHAT EXACTLY DOES A PAWNBROKER DO?
Or Myths Always Make A Better Story

COLLATERAL LENDING

Contrary to popular belief, a pawnbroker does not want to steal your stuff. In fact, unlike the energy, auto, and financial industries in America today, the pawnbroking industry is so extensively policed that it looks like a Catholic convent by comparison. A pawnbroker, first and foremost, lends money based on collateral. This is the main way that he derives income. As with any other credit, when the time comes to repay the loan, fees and interest are involved. He lends his customers money based on a percentage of his assessed value of whatever the person brings in. In addition, even though the loan is short term, there are still paperwork requirements—including reporting all collateral received (in great detail) to the police on a regular basis to avoid receipt of stolen items. This will naturally translate to a higher interest rate than a traditional bank loan, but alternatively provide a lending venue that is different from a bank, meets short-term lending needs that banks don't, and is available to a greater segment of society than banks.

STICKER SHOCK
or the price is right

Since a pawnbroker does not require credit, employment, or reference checks, he has to rely on what he can sell the collateral for in the event a customer doesn't redeem his loan ticket at the end of the loan period—typically three to six months. When storing and selling anything, inherent risks and costs are involved, especially for used items.

A lot of the negative feelings people have about pawnbrokers are a result of the difference between how the customer values his property versus the value the pawnbroker assigns to it. The borrowing or selling public probably feels pretty much the same way about realtors and prospective home buyers right now—a mixture of shock, dismay, and sometimes desperate horror. All of us can relate to a time when we wanted to sell something and were insulted by a "low-ball" offer. If it's just one so-called low offer, we shake our heads and rightfully comment on the greed and nerve of such a person. But if it's month after month and the house is sitting on the market without a single offer close to what you think its worth, we might start to panic. We might even start to label and blame whole groups of people.

And yet the only price we can sell something for is the price someone is willing to pay. When the demand for a particular item is high and the supply is limited, prices rise and the buyers complain while the sellers reap the rewards of the market. Even though this law of supply and demand is commonly known, often the "value" of an item is tied to personal rather than market meaning.

What is valuable to you may not have a commensurate retail value. Even retail values anymore are questionable with the closing of thousands of locations of big-box retailers in the US and overseas with inventories being liquidated at fire sale prices. MasterCard actually came out with a brilliant series of "priceless" commercials capitalizing on that very concept. Let's apply that using an example especially relevant in the current "housing crisis."

"Your House"

Cost to add that home theater: $50,000

The chance you'll recover that in this market: ZERO

*The memories of all your friends laughing
and crying over a good film: priceless*

The sixth sense of every good pawnbroker is in determining the fair market value of an item. This sixth sense is a very careful balancing act of what the current fair market value of the item is and if the item will tend to depreciate while in the pawnbroker's possession. While the pawnbroker wants to loan you as much money as they possibly can they must also keep in mind the non-recourse nature of the loan and their ability to be able to recover their investment plus a small profit should the pawn loan default.

TAKE YOUR STUFF BACK, PLEASE!

It is not, generally speaking, in the best interest of a pawnbroker to hang on to collateral and then try to sell it for a variety of reasons:

Market values fluctuate. The pawnbroker always faces the risk that the item will be worth less at the end of the loan period than when the customer brought it in. Of course, successful pawnbrokers are more adept at assessing that risk at the outset.

The credit business is more lucrative. Obviously, the profit margin on selling used merchandise is a lot lower than collecting interest and fees. There's always a story or two about a broker making a killing on a piece of collateral, but that's rare. Let's put it this way—you don't see Capital One and American Express taking in collateral. Banks hold mortgage and promissory notes on real property like houses and cars, but even *they* know that trying to recover your principal on a piece of collateral is difficult. Why do you think the bulk of your monthly payments in the first years of amortized bank loans are applied to interest?

Retail space is expensive. It takes a lot more prime commercial space to attractively display items for sale than to safely store it. Pawnbrokers have safe and secure areas to store valuables because they are responsible for having to replace an item if lost, stolen, or damaged, and certainly if they have to try to resell it in good condition if unclaimed. However, sales floor security is often much costlier because it is riskier.

Buy low, sell high works for stocks, not collateral. Pawnbrokers are not, by trade, investors. In other words, Warren Buffet is not a pawnbroker, and most pawn brokers are not Warren Buffet (well, at least as far as we know). Most of the used merchandise pawnbrokers lend on does not increase in value over time. Therefore, the incentive is for the borrower to redeem his collateral, not for the pawnbroker to hold on to it while it decreases in value.

GARAGE SALE JUNKIES

A pawnbroker is not a garage sale junkie waiting to find a Monet behind a black velvet Elvis painting. Don't expect a pawnshop to be able to loan you money on everything that you bring into the store. While the pawnbrokers want to loan you as much money as they can, they base the loan strictly on the fair market value of the item you pledged. The best property to pawn would be something that's easily valued, easily stored, and does not have a shelf life. This could include fine jewelry, coins and currency, high-grade firearms, and high-quality tools and musical instruments.

CHAPTER TWO

NEVER MIX POLITICS AND RELIGION
But Money And Religion Make A Fine Stew

IT'S IN THE BIBLE

The most commonly misunderstood concept in the Bible is that of lending money for interest. In the Old Testament, there are sections that clearly speak of this:

"If thou lend money to any of my people, even to the poor with thee, thou shalt not be to him as a creditor; neither shall ye lay upon him interest" (Exodus, 22:24 [Hebrew Bible, 1917]). *Translation: You can lend to any of your countrymen or ethnic group, even if they are poor, and you can't charge interest either on the money you can't lend.*

- "Thou shalt not lend upon interest to thy brother: interest of money, interest of victuals, interest of any thing that is lent upon interest. Unto a foreigner thou mayest lend upon interest; but unto thy brother thou shalt not lend upon interest; that the Lord thy God may bless thee in all that thou puttest thy hand unto, in the land whither thou goest in to possess it" (Deuteronomy 23:20-21). *Translation: You can lend to money to foreigners and charge interest, but not to your brother (whom you can't lend money to at all anyway). If you follow this rule, you will be successful in all your endeavors, including plundering and looting any land you go into.*

- "If thou lend money to any of my people that is poor by thee, thou shalt not be to him as a usurer, neither shalt thou lay upon him usury" (Exodus 22:25–27 [The Holy Bible, New King James Version, 1982]). *Translation: Okay, ignore what I said in Exodus 22:24—you can lend money to poor people, but you can't charge them interest.*

The early Christian and Jewish leaders forbade their constituents to lend money to others of the same religion, but it was not forbidden to extend loans with interest to those outside the faith. The Catholic Church took it a step further at various times during its history, completely prohibiting usury, but even then found ways around the prohibition when needed, parsing words worse than Bill Clinton. Depending on the year or sometimes even the month of the year, a "brother" could be considered a fellow parishioner or a stranger (and thus a potential lender).

Of course, not wanting to appear hypocritical, the good church elders convened secretly with the mercantile economists of the day and devised many clever mechanisms to provide loopholes even during prohibition.

One of the earliest ways to disguise interest was within an exchange rate. Since a wide range of currencies existed, monetary exchange was both necessary and complex. "The interest element in such dealings [was] normally hidden by the nature of the transactions either in foreign exchange or as bills of exchange or, frequently, as both."[5]

At other times, the church and civil authorities simply turned to Jewish lenders or called the interest "administrative fees" to finance their wars or trade. The need for cash flow simply outweighed the moral prohibitions both sought to invoke.

They also ignored the New Testament allowances for usury (The Holy Bible, New King James Version, 1982):

- "Thou oughtest therefore to have put my money to the exchangers, and then at my coming I should have received mine own with usury" (Matthew 25:27). *Translation:You should have invested my money with the money lenders so I could have earned interest.*

- "Wherefore then gavest not thou my money into the bank, that at my coming I might have required mine own with usury?" (Luke 19:23) *Translation: Or if not with the moneylenders, the banks—so I could have earned interest.*

In fact, Matthew 25 clearly condemns the "unprofitable" servant and rewards the "good and faithful" servant who prospered, turning five "talents" into ten (The Holy Bible, New King James Version, 1982):

---

5.   Glyn Davies, *A History of Money from Ancient Times to the Present Day*, 3rd. ed. (Cardiff: University of Wales Press, 2002).

- "And he that had received the five talents coming, brought other five talents, saying: Lord, thou didst deliver to me five talents. Behold I have gained other five over and above. His lord said to him: Well done, good and faithful servant, because thou hast been faithful over a few things, I will place thee over many things. Enter thou into the joy of thy lord" (Matthew 25: 20–21). *Translation: That's a better return than Wall Street, Bernard Madoff, or Lehman Brothers—sign me up.*

- "But he that had received the one talent, came and said: Lord, I know that thou art a hard man; thou reapest where thou hast not sown and gatherest where thou hast not strewed. And being afraid, I went and hid thy talent in the earth. Behold here thou hast that which is thine. And his lord answering, said to him: Wicked and slothful servant, thou knewest that I reap where I sow not and gather where I have not strewed. Thou oughtest therefore to have committed my money to the bankers: and at my coming I should have received my own with usury. Take ye away therefore the talent from him and give it him that hath ten talents. For to every one that hath shall be given, and he shall abound: but from him that hath not, that also which he seemeth to have shall be taken away. And the unprofitable servant, cast ye out into the exterior darkness. There shall be weeping and gnashing of teeth" (Matthew 25:24–30). *Translation: There's no welfare for the lazy.*

Why would Christianity specifically exclude these lessons? Is it because it fosters the (pre-capitalist) idea that hard work and investment should be rewarded, while laziness should be punished? Instead the church seems to extend the Old Testament's prohibiting usury amongst brothers to a pre-communist/socialist "universal brotherhood." In other words, take from those who have and give to those who are needy, without regard for the productivity or investment that created wealth or the lack thereof of the "have-nots."

Perhaps the churches wanted the controlling factor of poverty. Just as the idea that birth control is inherently evil keeps hordes of third world families in abject poverty, arbitrarily shutting down access to lending facilities keeps the poor dependent on the church for charity, which then translates to power and influence. It's similar to welfare's self-destructive cycle of dependency, which is far more debilitating in the long run than a short-term high interest rate or even, in most instances, the loss of the collateral.

Other ideas propounded that "the usurer sells nothing to the borrower that belongs to him. He sells only time, which belongs to God. He can therefore not make a profit from selling someone else's property."[6] And "the usurer acts contrary to natural law, for he sells time, which is common to all creatures."[7] This idea, while so lofty it strains credulity, ignores the reality that human societies depend on money to actually live. It is the fuel of life, only because it is a medium by which we exchange our labor, our goods, and our ideas and the measure by which we secure our futures. It also ignores the reality that not all human endeavors are successful, and that lenders should be compensated for the risk of lending the fuel that secures their future.

LOMBARDI AND MEDICI VERSUS FREDDIE MAC & FANNIE MAE

Ironically, the pawnshops of Renaissance Italy were prosperous in large part because of the papacy, who used their services. The Medici family had a reputation for reliability and honesty. Giovanni di Bicci de' Medici rose from humble beginnings, building his property business into a successful commercial endeavor and then branching into the pawnbroking/banking business, which he expanded throughout the northern Italian city-states in the Lombardy region, and then all of Europe. (Martinelli) The use of the term "Lombard" for a reliable pawnshop grew slowly from city to city and became prevalent in Cahors, southern France. The words Cahorsine and Lombard soon became synonymous with pawnbroking. The Medici family was so closely tied with the Vatican that one of their family members became Pius IV (Giovanni Angelo Medici), the pope from 1559 to 1565 (Martinelli). Of course, the appointment probably didn't command as high a price as the Illinois senate seat in 2008.

This kind of nepotism and insider deal making is not a foreign concept to most Americans. We need look no further than the Freddie Mac/Fannie Mae debacle that will clearly cost U.S. citizens dearly to see the evidence of it. Unfortunately, the names of the people running this enterprise are not nearly as reputable as the Medici name.[8] The same types of elites who point the finger at pawnbrokers for "exploiting" the lower class still do not understand the risks associated with lending to people with limited means. Worse than that, whole "respect-

6. Jeremy Rifkin, *The European Dream* (Cambridge: Polity, 2004).
7. Odd Langholm, *Aristotelian Analysis of Usury* (Bergen: Universitetsforlaget, 1985).
8. On December 18, 2006, U.S. regulators filed 101 civil charges against chief executive Franklin Raines; chief financial officer J. Timothy Howard; and the former controller Leanne G. Spencer.

able" industries colluded with Freddie Mac/Fannie Mae to lie or otherwise convince these borrowers with unclear loan terms that they could actually afford to borrow as much as they did. And why should these liberal elites bother to understand the risk? Even while they were taking enormous profits and bonuses, at the end of the day they did *not* have to swallow the risk—the American taxpayer does. You can be sure that those responsible for this mess are not the ones losing their homes or paying for it at a rate commensurate to the profits they took.

It is refreshing to see that venerable institutions that are the fete of Washington elites because of their supposedly enlightened ideals in extending home ownership and borrowing opportunities to low-income people were, in reality, concerned only with their own profits. These respectable lenders collected enormous (and unjustified, given the failures of the industry) salaries, perks, and bonuses, which amounted to a huge "fee" and high interest rate on each dollar loaned on money that wasn't even wholly theirs to lend.

In comparison, the pawnbroking industry is a far better deal for low-income borrowers. Even though no one borrows from a pawnbroker to buy a home, the point is that these "respectable" lenders are touted as social idealists working to help low-income families. In reality the red tape and bureaucratic layers they surrounded themselves with served to conceal the fraud and deception they wielded for personal benefit.

FANNIE MAE & FREDDIE MAC	PAWN INDUSTRY
Hidden high interest & fees.	High interest stated up front in easy to understand terms.
Risk is assumed by the American taxpayers.	Risk assumed by pawn broker.
Interest paid by borrower up front during term of loan.	Interest paid only when collateral redeemed.
If loan unpaid, recourse is: • foreclosure on collateral • can sue for costs, fees, unpaid interest, and difference in principle, if any, upon sale of collateral • negative credit reporting	If loan unpaid, recourse is sale of collateral.

THE FRANCISCAN LOOPHOLE

As mentioned earlier, church officials frequently manipulated and selectively enforced the usury laws to bolster the financial power of the church. When it wanted to keep its own borrowing cost low, the church enforced the usury prohibition. Also, the harsh condemnations of the church conveniently enhanced their wealth as many moneylenders, seeking holy absolution, attempted to buy it by building large, ornate churches and donating substantial sums of money. This was a true "pay to play" arrangement that eventually garnered more favorable religious treatment toward lending in various Franciscan circles. At other times, the church *itself* readily loaned money for interest. Franciscan monks— who glorified poverty as being holy even while extracting huge payoffs from wealthy lenders—decided they wanted better control of their constituency's limited incomes. Generously proclaiming it a necessary service, they became some of the earliest moneylenders, offering carefully disguised interest-bearing loans throughout the Middle Ages.

THE MONEY CHANGERS

As discussed earlier, the moneychangers in biblical times served two purposes to handle the complex monetary exchanges and to loan money. Any interests or fees they charged were incorporated within the exchange rate.

An example of a loan in this context would be:

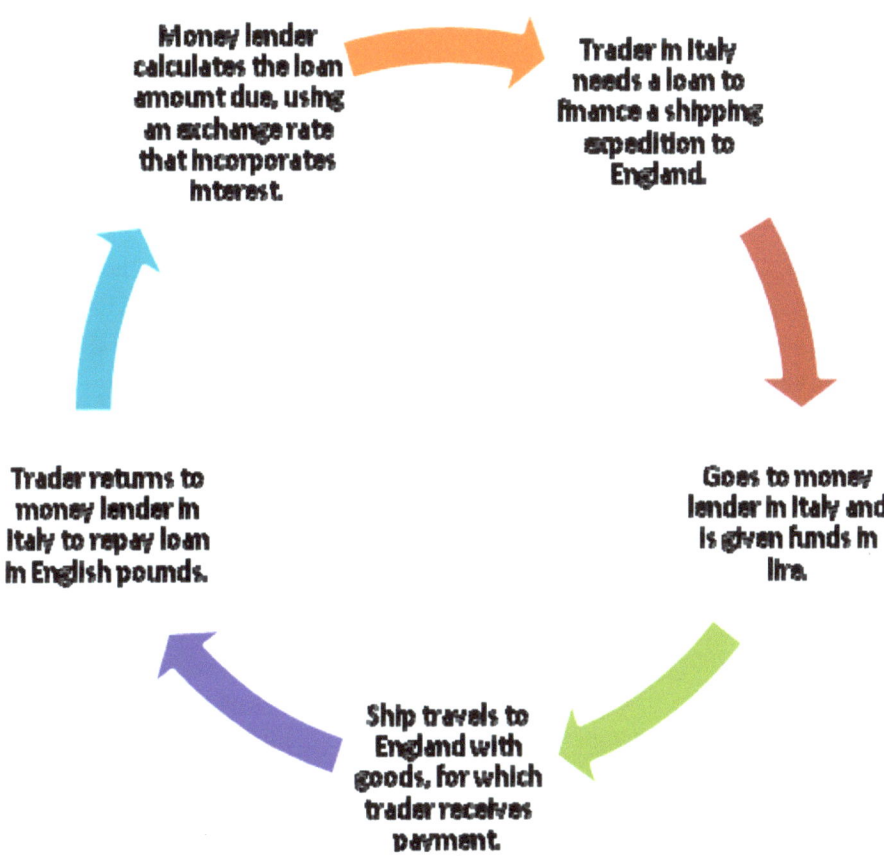

Money lender calculates the loan amount due, using an exchange rate that incorporates interest.

Trader in Italy needs a loan to finance a shipping expedition to England.

Goes to money lender in Italy and is given funds in lira.

Ship travels to England with goods, for which trader receives payment.

Trader returns to money lender in Italy to repay loan in English pounds.

The moneychangers of Jesus's time exchanged Antiochian tetradrachms for the local currency (shekels), exacting a fee between 4 and 8 percent for their services. The story where Jesus overturned their tables because he didn't feel the gates of the temple were the right place to conduct that business is an example of the church's hypocritical views toward the money changers. In fact, such moneychangers set up

shop there as a service, to deal with people who came to pay their half shekel temple tax, which the rabbis insisted be paid in silver didrachms of Tyre, which nobody carried. These taxes were collected and used for worthwhile purposes, not any different from church tithes:

> "Part of the money was used to pay for the communal sacrifices, the incense and showbread, the red cow and the scapegoat, the priestly garments, the libations accompanying ownerless sacrifices, the inspection of sacrifices for blemishes, the teaching of the sacrificial laws, and scribes and criminal courts in Jerusalem. The rest was used to repair the Temple and the city; if any remained it was used to buy animal burnt- offerings."[9]

Convenience fees were apparently only morally acceptable if the religious institutions collected them themselves. At least the temple money changer fees were clearly stated up front; they were only taking advantage of the fact that the temple itself set up an arcane system demanding certain types of coins for tithing.

Like the temple tax, today's banking fees are virtually unavoidable. But unlike the temple tax, there are so many different types of banking fees it's difficult to accurately figure the "percentage" we are paying on using our own money. We are pushed to participate in a system that charges us often outrageous interest rates, sometimes without consent. For example, when we use our debit

---

9.   Rosenfeld, Azriel, Rabbi Dr., *Halacha Overview: The Temple Tax*, Torah.org, 2006.

cards and unwittingly draw over the limit (easy to do if there is more than one person/card on the account), our cards are not refused for insufficient funds. Instead, we are automatically charged an average over limit fee of $39 on the "loan." With many merchants not accepting checks, we don't even have time to realize we're over the limit and run to deposit sufficient funds. That $2 cup of joe could end up costing you $41, at an interest rate of 2050 percent. But of course the pawnbrokers, who show you your fees up front that you consent to, are still considered on par with the evil money changers.

AL-RAHN
or profit the prophet's way?

Like the Christian and Jewish pawnbrokers before them, many Indonesian Pegadaian pawn branches offer an Islamic service where an administration fee is charged and a complex tariff formula used to avoid charges of usury.

The Qu'ran also distinguishes between trade, partnerships (participatory financing), and usury. The main difference is based on the concept of risk sharing. While Islam specifically prohibits charging interest on money, it does not prohibit a person with capital, who plays no further part in a project, from sharing the profit with the entrepreneur. If the project ends in profit, they share the profit according to agreement. If it results in loss, the financier bears the capital loss, and the entrepreneur has lost the benefit of his time and effort, which was his part of the investment.[10]

Although the term "profit" is used to describe the lender's return on money lent rather than the word "interest," in reality this type of lending is very similar to pawnbroking. Both parties share some level of risk. Unlike bank collateralized lending, where the bank can recover any losses between the value of the collateral and what it sells for, as well as a whole host of onerous fees and the costs of selling the collateral, pawnbrokers truly assume the risk of their participation in the transaction. If the loan is not paid off, the pawnbroker keeps and sells the collateral and does not collect any interest at all on the loan. If the collateral sells for less than the loan amount, the pawnbroker has no further recourse against the borrower. In fact, if that borrower were to come again looking for a loan and

---

10.   A. L. M. Abdul Gafoor, "Mudaraba-based Investment and Finance," Appropriate Technology Foundation, Groningen, The Netherlands.

offered additional collateral, the pawnbroker would not shun the borrower or deem him not to be creditworthy.

Of course, credit reporting is a lucrative business on its own. Negative credit reporting is a risk-free way for banks to shame the borrower into paying on time and to also unilaterally raise interest rates to astronomical levels. Akin to loan-sharking enforcement, the punishment for even a day late on a credit report can be severe and costly.

CHAPTER THREE

A LONG HISTORY
Or Some Things Never Change

Most pawnbroker information states that pawnbrokering began with the Chinese about three thousand years ago. However, if we understand that pawnbrokering is just a form of collateralized lending, we see that, in fact, the history extends further back than this. Beginning with the Bronze Age, over five thousand years ago, human societies had reached a point of complexity and interaction where a system of economics or rudimentary accounting needed to be and was developed. We know about this because of the historical source materials found that document the current events as well as recording prior oral history and customs.

The fact is, life throws some punches you can't dodge sometimes. Having the ability to borrow money—whether on your reputation or on the stuff you own—makes surviving those down times a little bit easier. Of course, pawnbroking made it easier *and* faster to get the money needed, and (despite its reputation) has offered a valuable service to society for thousands of years. Throughout the world, emerging economies used various shades of collateralized lending— from pawnbroking to money changing—before more sophisticated formal banking systems ever developed.

Religious and governmental leaders often condemned and prohibited these collateralized lending institutions, which provided access to cash flow from paupers to popes to kings. Monetary need and practical reality simply outweighed esoteric or moral arguments against charging interest on loans (usury). Regardless of the country, successful pawnbrokers often used their money and proximity to power to either gain positions in government or otherwise positively influence perceptions toward the practice of usury.

As formal banking institutions took hold and catered to the upper- and middle-income classes, public perception toward usury changed. Charging interest became an accepted cost of everyday life and business. Borrowing money from a bank or using a credit card became an everyday occurrence of convenience, not just a necessary transaction to get by from week to week.

Pawnbrokers continued, as they do today, to provide necessary cash flow to the working poor. The industry that once was condemned for merely charging interest now battled class prejudice. Then as banks and credit card companies began casting their nets for more customers, dipping down into the working class, pawnbrokers were suddenly demonized for "exploiting" their uneducated, low-income customers.

Lured by the perception of a higher class status of credit cards and even home ownership, and the ruthless marketing ploys of initially affordable interest rates and barely understandable borrowing terms, vast numbers of people eagerly signed on only to find themselves in far over their heads shortly thereafter. Suddenly "Uncle" pawnbroker does not seem so undesirable, and his terms far fairer than the suited banker, mortgage broker, or gold card logo.

Getting to where we are today is a trip back in time and around the world. And yet, the story revolves around the control of money and the manipulation of public perception as the necessity arose. Some things, whether in Bronze Age Babylon or electronic age Washington, D.C., never change. The rest of this chapter will be a whirlwind tour from over five thousand years ago to present day, tracking the footprints of the pawn industry over time and continents.

BRONZE AGE BANKERS
the sumerians (4000–1200 BC).

The earliest known people of Mesopotamia in the "cradle of civilization" or "fertile crescent" area surrounding the Euphrates and Tigris rivers also created the earliest known form of writing (cuneiform). Cuneiform writing entailed using a sharp tool (stylus) on clay tablets, and archaeologists have uncovered Sumerian clay tablets detailing collateralized lending transactions as far back as the early

Bronze Age. Interestingly enough, the fires of hell weren't depicted underneath the lending figures. That took a bit more sophisticated mechanism of greed to equate lending to evil.

BABYLONIAN EMPIRE (1728–1686 BC)

King Hammurabi ruled over the Babylonian Empire during the height of its power and influence (1795–1750 BC), incorporating and expanding upon the Sumerian culture in Mesopotamian region during the Bronze Age. He was responsible for creating the first known written laws. Called the Code of Hammurabi, it contains 150 paragraphs pertaining to loans, interest, pledges and guarantees, and standardizing procedures. The code was carved on eight-foot high black stone, and references are made to preceding laws that substantiate the evidence found in fragments of clay tablets.[11] Prominently displaying the rules of lending kept it fair and transparent. Perhaps our courts and legislators might do well to spend some of the billions in bailout dollars to commission a piece of sculpture that does the same. They could use some of the workers unceremoniously downsized out of companies that went belly-up to carve the words, but the FCC might have a moral problem with some of the epithets drawn. And of course the CEOs who were kept on at places like AIG and Lehman Brothers are far too busy to do the work, since they already have taxpayer paid poolside conferences to attend.

The Bible provides relevant source material of historical social customs and structures both be-

> *Fast forward 5000 years or so and the pendulum swings the other way… the people are bailing out the ruling class.*

fore and after the inception of three largest monotheistic religions of Christianity, Judaism, and Islam. The Old Testament is shared by all three of these religions, and further, it records the pagan rituals preceding the concept of one God. We know from biblical texts that during the Bronze Age in Mesopotamia that people borrowed by putting up collateral even then. Prior to the biblical laws of Leviticus and Deuteronomy, in fact, the rulers of these Mesopotamian lands instituted a "clean slates" program where pledged (pawned) collateral that had

---

11.   Horne, Charles, *Code of Hammurabi*, The Encyclopaedia Britannica, 11th ed, 1915.

been or were about to be forfeited were returned to the debtor[12] making current bankruptcy laws seem miserly at best and yet completely unfair to the creditors who were left empty-handed. In all likelihood, however, these seemingly charitable acts were probably implemented to avoid uprisings and class strife, and to inspire loyalty from newly conquered subjects.[13] The earliest record of debt cancellation was initiated by Enmetena in Sumer, Mesopotamia, around 2400 BC after his victory over the neighboring city of Umma.[14]

Today we are similarly bullied by fear of plant closings and dire economic consequences, forcing our leaders to lend our money to companies like Ford, Chrysler, GM, Citibank, Washington Mutual, AIG, etc. Credit ratings and failed business models are irrelevant for evaluating the risk of these borrowers. Although these "loans" are supposedly "highly collateralized" (per Senator Barney Frank and his cohorts), we are only taking the borrower's word on the worth of said collateral. And the fees for administering these loans, as well as the salaries of the "Car Czar" and his assistants, are not being paid for by the borrowers. In comparison, the "clean slates" program available for the majority of struggling Americans is the onerous bankruptcy laws that these now-failed financial institutions pushed our Congress to pass in 2005. These same institutions that demonize pawn brokers for "preying" on poor people continue their gluttonous returns on money that doesn't even belong to them.

---

12.   Hudson, Dr. Michael, The Lost Tradition of Biblical Debt Cancellations , published by Henry George School of Social Science (New York City). ©1993.
13.   Vronsky and Westerman, *12,000 Years of Elliot Waves*, 1999, http://www.gold-eagle.com/editorials_99/mbutler120299d.html.
14.   Wegerif, Boudewijn, *Truth from Mesopotamia,* Buckfastleigh, Devon, July, 2007.

An Inconvenient Pawn Ticket:

Ancient Sumerian Cuneiform Tablet Detailing a Loan for Silver

from The Money Museum at the Banca D'Italia

THE POWER OF PERCEPTION
and the meaning of profit

ANCIENT GREECE AND ROME – IT ALL DEPENDS ON WHO YOU ARE

On the cusp of the Roman Empire's conversion to Christianity between 382 and 391, there is evidence of the pagan ministries being involved in issuing loans on collateral. Amongst the writings of Quintus Aurelius Symmachus, a pagan prominent in Rome's political circles, he complains to Emperor Valentinian II about the Christian clerics hitting up rich elderly Romans, enticing them to leave their estates to the church instead of their heirs. The clerics were using the antipagan laws to invalidate monies left to the pagan "Vestal Virgins" and the "ministers of the gods," who had received grant money from the state for "maintenance and sensible privileges" until "some degenerate money-broker turned the fund into a collateral for loans to porters and sewage cleaners."[15]

Again we see that as long as the money is going to the "right people"—whether pagan or Christian—then it is morally acceptable to the elite religious, social, and political leaders. Anyone who mainly lends to the poor and working class is deemed degenerate. After all, "maintenance and sensible privileges" for the "right people" is far more important than feeding lowly porters or sewage cleaners and their families. The king and the priest must be paid first.

CHINA – BUDDHA APPROVED BUT MAO DIDN'T

Collateralized lending is believed to have been a part of China's long history since at least the Southern Song dynasty which began in 1127. The region of Huizhou did not have a surplus of farmland, so the people there would send their children at age twelve to apprentice with businesses and traders in town.

The Huizhou operated in many different businesses from tea trading, restaurants, and pottery to the reportedly most prosperous areas of salt trading and pawnbroking. They expanded their services throughout Asia, using their profits to fund scholarly pursuits which then established their positions within the reigning dynasties.

> *Even today the pawn broking industry literature, such as Today's Pawnbroker, National Pawnbroker, and various state association journals recognize that efforts need to be made to achieve recognition of industry respectability and to shed the negative stereotype.*

Like the European pawnbrokers in the Middle Ages, the Huizhou used their money to gain influence in the Ming dynasty and a presence in the cultural elite that actually helped marry the virtues of Confucianism with the concepts of business. The Huizhou were able to change the perception of their industry from that of "usurious pawnbroking, exorbitant luxury, sexual voracity, and litigation" to one of "thrift, honesty, and effort".[16] They influenced the traditional Confucian ideas that all profit was negative to one where profitable activities that were a benefit to the society as well were a natural condition of economic activity. As

15.   Michael Sympson, *Keeping the Faith,* 4/26/2008.

16.   Brook, Timothy, Luong, Hy V. , *Culture and Economy: The Shaping of Capitalism in Eastern Asia,* University of Michigan Press, 1997.

such, Ming scholars began to accept the Huizhou and their business activities as a part of and not outside Confucian ideology.

The Buddhist monks further recognized the positive image achieved. Freed from the idea that business was somehow a less than noble pursuit, the monasteries established a number of enterprises that then financed the expansion into money lending and pawnbroking. This did not remove the Buddhist influence from the culture and, in fact, allowed the increased exposure and significance of Buddhist art and stories.[17]

Pawnbroking was a vital part of the Chinese culture until Mao and Communism took root and the state completely took over all financial and business institutions.[18] Like the Christian churches, Mao and Communism degraded rewarding individual effort and hard work in favor of a "brotherly" system that "spread the wealth". Karl Marx's famous axiom of "from each, according to his ability; to each, according to his need" paved the way for a state entity that controlled the flow of money. Although propounding atheism, the Mao state was just the flip side of religious institutions in that it's ultimate goal was to control the masses by a few elite. Although promises of heavenly reward and earthly quality may seem appalling to those who are down and out at the moment, in truth most people have an innate desire to build their successes on their own abilities and hard work. There are only three types of people who will continue to support such a system:

- Those who are either forced by a system that denies access to that opportunity (either by class, gender, religious, or racial status)

- Those who are by nature dependent, lazy, or mentally/physically incapable

- The elites in positions of power.

Although capitalism can produce inequities and unfairness, the idea itself is not corrupt but some individuals within it who seek to steal or deny access to power and money. Pawnbrokers, by setting up a "fair trade" system of collateral lending that extends access to money to even the lowest income class, actually promotes

17. Christie Hoerneman, "The Major Dynasties of China: Part I," 7/15/2008.

18. Gonzalez, Michael, *Informal Finance: Encouraging the Entrepreneurial Spirit in Post-Mao China*, http://www.heritage.org/Index/chapters/pdf/Index2006_Chap4.pdf.

individual endeavor and the ideals of capitalism more than traditional financial institutions.

JAPAN – THE SWORD CUTS BOTH WAYS

As trade expanded rapidly in Japan in the Kamakura era at the end of the twelfth century, the Japanese monks began engaging in pawnbroking and money lending, an integral segment of the developing banking industry in Japan just as it was in Europe. Village administrations in the eighteenth century modeled these earlier banking systems by establishing a "depository" that "offered loans and stored goods and promises of future goods."[19]

The samurai, or warrior caste, of Japan, who were originally peasants and land-owners, were soon brought into the monetization of the Japanese society by the elite castes they served. Required to live within fortifications now that these castes were building walled cities to protect themselves from canon fire, the samurai leased their land to rice farmers. Having no math skills, they had to turn to the "lowest and most contemned of social groups the outcast etas alone excepted money lenders and merchants" to handle the money transactions. Marriage or partnerships brought these merchants into alliances with samurai families to handle the complex money transactions.[20]

Again the common theme is that in an effort to maintain control over access to power, money, and social status, the elite class castigates anyone who dares threaten that system by extending that access. Ironically, the burdensome bureaucracy and class prejudice of traditional elitist institutions actually negate the unfavorable propaganda toward the pawnbroking industry. People still have to survive, and pawnbrokers help overcome obstacles by providing easy, necessary access to money that is otherwise denied.

---

19.   Volume 4. Early Modern Japan. Edited by John Whitney Hall and James L. McClain, assistant editor. 1991. pp.xxviii + 831.
20.   Origins of the Modern Japanese State – Selected Writings of E.H. Norman. Edited by John W. Dower. Edited with an introduction on E. H. Norman, "Japan and the Uses of History," by John W. Dower, Pantheon Books, Random House, New York, 1975.

<u>Thomas Mattman, Department of Mathematics and Statistics, California</u>
<u>State University</u>

YEARS OF MARRYING THE SAMURAI CASTE TO THE PAWNBROKER
CASTE YIELDS THE FIRST SAMURAI MATHEMATICIAN IN THE 21ST
CENTURY

EUROPE AND ENGLAND – CHURCHES AND KINGS

Following the conquest of William the Conqueror in 1066, the "House of Lombard" was established as a medieval bank and pawnbroker in England, expanding the Italian monetary systems. Although pawn lending was historically

used as a resource for the lowest working classes and the royalty, medieval records document the use of pawnbroker services by a variety of the "middle" class
as well, often to further entrepreneurial endeavors, and by low-level church
officials to sustain their existence:

- In 1173, Jocelin de Brakelond, a monk of Edmundsbury, details the
  pledging of "silk vestments and gold vessels and other ornaments" of the
  church by the other monks and the Abbot Hugh in order to sustain the
  abbey.[21]

- In 1199, two traders from Marseilles contracted with two lenders in
  Messina to finance a shipping venture. In return for "1,600 tarins of gold
  (Messina weight) weighing fifty-three and a third ounces, at the risk of
  God and the sea; for which, by a secure contract, we agree to give you
  in Provence fifty-five solidi in royal crowns of Marseilles for each ounce,
  i.e., the sum of ,146.13s.3d". The two traders "put in pledge" 141 pigs,
  four sacks of gall nuts, fifteen bundles of licorice wood, and five bundles
  of soft leather as collateral against the loan.[22]

Early in the thirteenth century, these capitalist Christian bankers from Italy (and
the Cahorsins/ Caursines, the southern France branch of the Lombard family)
not only officiated as "papal brokers" but also catered to all the "rich and pow-
erful in society." Although used by virtually everyone in England involved in
trade or politics, pawnbrokers still faced the negative Aristotelian concepts of
money lending and interest. Many medieval scholars accused them of "cloaking
their usury under the show of trade, and pretending not to know that whatever
is added to the principal is usury."[23] This did not stop King Edward III from using

---

21. Medieval Sourcebook: Jocelin de Brakelond: Chronicle of The Abbey of St. Edmund's
(1173–1202).

22. From: L. Blancard, ed, Documents Inédits sur le Commerse de Marseille au Moyen Age,
(Marseilles: Barlatier-Feissat, Pere et Fils, 1884), Vol. 1, p. 3, reprinted in Roy C. Cave & Herbert
H. Coulson, A Source Book for Medieval Economic History, (Milwaukee: The Bruce Publishing
Co., 1936; reprint ed., New York: Biblo & Tannen, 1965), pp. 105–106. Scanned by Jerome S.
Arkenberg, Cal. State Fullerton. The text has been modernized by Prof. Arkenberg.

23. From: Matthew of Paris, English History, trans. J. A. Giles, (London: H. G. Bohn, 1849),
Vol. I, p.2; reprinted in Roy C. Cave & Herbert H. Coulson, eds., A Source Book for Medieval
Economic History, (Milwaukee: The Bruce Publishing Co., 1936; reprint ed., New York: Biblo
& Tannen, 1965), pp. 179–180. Scanned by Jerome S. Arkenberg, Cal. State Fullerton. The text
has been modernized by Prof. Arkenberg.

their services to finance the English war with France, pawning the royal crown jewels for collateral. Apparently he realized what the scholars in their ivory towers did not—money helps make things happen easier than pretty prose.

In the late Middle Ages (1487–1577), the Fuggers, a prominent German banking family (later they changed their name to Rothschild), replaced the Medici and in fact gained control of England's silver production as collateral on loans to the royal family. Desperately looking for ways to extend the collateral they used to future tax payments, the Bank of England was established. In particular, Charles Montagu, First Lord of the Treasury and Chancellor of the Exchequer, needed to pay for the wartime expenses of William III. The loan was presented along with the bank charter in 1694 and was approved to be paid at an annual interest rate of 6 percent against the collateral of the Crown's ships' tonnage and liquor duties.[24] This is a concept that the US government is using today to buttress industries that have been plundered by the wealthy looters who run them. The costs of the foibles of the minority elite class are always pressed upon the shoulders of the rest of the citizenry, even in a so-called capitalist democracy.

In the late seventeenth century the Englishman Francis Child, took over the goldsmith banking shop the "Marygold" and expanded into banking services that accepted deposits, which he in turn loaned, maintaining fractional reserves. The Marygold was still involved in pawn arrangements with the borrower securing the loan with plate, jewelry, or a penal bond, reflecting the traditional aspect of goldsmiths acting as pawnbrokers, even while regularly making loans with no mention of collateral. Child may have been the first to introduce lending to customers in the form of overdrafts, ranging from twenty-five to thirty-five thousand pounds at any time.

Instead of letting the negative perception of pawnbrokers limit him, Childs used his business to become a major participant in financing the government war debt, which he then parlayed into advancing his political and social position, much like the Chinese Huizhou. He was knighted in 1689, became sheriff of London in 1690, and the prime warden of the Goldsmiths' Company in 1691.[25] Even with the establishment of the Bank of England and Dutch merchant

---

24. "Money and Culture", edited by Hans-Walter Hannisa and Fiona Cox, Peter Lang Verlag, München, 2007

25. Stephen Quinn, "Tallies or Reserves? Sir Francis Child's Balance Between Capital Reserves and Extending Credit to the Crown, 1685–1695," University of Illinois, Champaign-Urbana.

banking, most loans were still collateralized loans,[26] and Child played a part in countering the negative image of pawnbrokers by bridging the perceptual divide between "banks" and "pawn shops."

INDONESIA – ADAPTATION IS KEY TO SURVIVAL

Pawnbrokers did not operate as small mom-and-pop shops in Indonesia. Instead they came to represent an ongoing battle for monetary control between the great colonial powers of the Dutch and the English. For many years, the Dutch banking colonialists eschewed the British banking snobbery, recognizing the profit opportunities of pawnbrokering, operating within a complete monopoly on the islands of Indonesia.

When the British were in control of the Dutch East Indies in the early nineteenth century, Governor Raffles reversed the monopoly the Dutch Bank van Leening had on pawnbrokering, enabling British entrepreneurs to establish a foothold in the Indonesia pawn market. However, when the Dutch returned to power in 1816, they attempted to reverse the British free market system. It took them until 1901 to reestablish the state monopoly system that is still in effect today, even though Indonesia is no longer under Dutch colonial rule (Graham 2007).

To accommodate a majority Islamic population, the pawnbroking industry contorted itself with bureaucratic red tape that serves to disguise the interest charged as administrative fees. Ironically, this is not substantively different from how the early Christian church and Jewish temples created money-changing mechanisms to circumvent religious laws against usury. It seems that hard as we try to differentiate ourselves by religion, when it comes to money good ideas translate well.

MEXICO AND SOUTH AMERICA – A LESSON IN SPIN

The power to manipulate perception is clearest when we see what happens when an idea is taken, like twin babies, and inserted into different cultures. Whereas kings and popes and noble castes twisted the perception of an already established economic tool in early Europe, England, the Middle East, and Asia, the idea of

---

26. Dr. Michael Hudson, "The Creditary/Monetarist Debate in Historical Perspective" (presented at the New School, New York, 1999).

pawnbroking in Mexico and South America never suffered the tawdry image as a "lender of last resort" since it was officially sanctioned from its inception.

Mexico. In Mexico, the Monte de Piedad, or National Pawnshop, was established as a respected government institution. In 1775 Charles III of Spain authorized the owner of one of the richest silver mines in Mexico to develop it as a solution for the working class cash flow problems. Originally named the "Sacred and Royal Mountain of Pity of Souls" (El Sacro y Real Monte de Piedad de Animas), it began with a chapel on site.

The Monte de Piedad originally applied its profits to charitable works and also helped provide a venue for small artisans and businessmen to sell their wares.[27] Today it successfully continues as a profitable institution that still provides necessary access in an often cash-strapped economy, as well as a venue for antique hunters from wealthier patrons. What a difference the right "spin" can make on how a whole culture perceives an idea!

REDEFINING OPPORTUNITIES FOR PROFIT
anything goes in america

QUAKERS – PROFITING FROM A PERCEPTION OF TRUST

In the eighteenth century United States, many pawnbrokers, doubling as shipping agents, were Quakers who were unhindered by the hypocritical religious arguments against usury in this New World. In keeping with English tradition, the pawnshops were often called Lombard houses, and since the shipping trade was so often a customer, most major port cities in America still have a Lombard Street or Lombard Alley. Quakers were the Lombards of the New World—trustworthy lenders to the working class and merchants alike.

Of course all the major cities in this new country developed near ports because of the need for proximity to transportation for goods and travelers. They were also centers of population for the working class, and pawnbrokers flourished as they provided access to money not readily available both because of their class status and simply because the very few banking institutions there were catered to the merchant and upper class.

---

27.   MONTE DE PIEDAD: More than Household Finance, By Jennifer j. rose, 1997.

PROVIDENT LOAN – PROFITS CLOAKED IN LIBERAL DISGUISE

During the financial panic of 1893, there were few, if any, social and government agencies to help the poor. The only readily available option was the high-interest loans from pawnbrokers. As a brilliant public relations ploy, some of New York City's wealthiest and most unscrupulously vicious business leaders established a nonprofit pawnshop that offered low-interest short-term loans to individuals upon pledge of personal property.[28]

Thus the elite of New York, including J.P. Morgan and Cornelius Vanderbilt, became involved in the age-old pawnbroking business, competing for working-class dollars by presenting a cheaper alternative in the existing market. This was a calculated business move on their part, not a charitable one. It also marked the beginning of the elitist wealthy leaders using arguments of class exploitation to expand into the profits that banking to the great numbers of working-class people offered. The brilliant maneuver of creating a monster of pawnbrokers, who had heretofore been the working man's only resource, and painting themselves as the liberal-minded protectors served the robber barons well:

- It misdirected negative attention from their ruthless roles in the financial crisis.

- It gave them an opportunity to appear beneficent even while profiting.

- It expanded profit-making opportunities for the upper class by cloaking themselves as a "friend" to the working class as opposed to the unapproachable and mistrusted traditional banks.

The Provident Loan Society is still in operation, providing loans up to $50,000 for up to six months and for a substantially lower rate than other New York State pawnbrokers.[29] It even inspired the creation of the San Francisco Provident Loan Association, which works exclusively with jewelry, fine art, wine, and collectibles.

---

28. The Provident Loan Society of New York, http://www.providentloan.com/provident-history.shtml.
29. The Provident Loan Society of New York, http://www.providentloan.com/provident-history.shtml.

WINNING SOLUTIONS IN THE WILD WEST

Americans are known for their ingenuity in the face of obstacles. One fine example of this is the Salt River Project, which turned to collateralized lending to obtain financing for water reclamation projects in Arizona, one of which was the Theodore Roosevelt Dam. After having been refused loans from conventional lenders as "too risky," state representatives were able to push through legislation in 1902 with the support of newly elected President Roosevelt, which allowed local organizations to put up land as collateral to borrow money from the federal government for these projects. These water storage and delivery projects enabled America to expand and establish stronger and larger footholds in the western frontier.[30] Without the foresight, ingenuity, and shared risk taking of lenders like pawnbrokers to foster the very spirit of frontiersmen and women, we might not have ever had the great expanse that America is today.

Even Native Americans in the Southwest frequently made use of finely crafted silver jewelry as collateral against loans at trading posts, which often operated as pawnshops. Mutual distrust kept most, if not all, American Indians from using the few traditional banking institutions that took hold in the Southwest. Having jewelry available to pawn at regular seasonal periods, linked to harvest and hunting activities, was an important and respectable part of the economic and social life of Native American tribes.[31] Since the jewelry was often used in summer dances and ceremonials, pawn activity would also be scheduled so they could be redeemed in time for these events. Again, without the equal lending opportunities that collateral-based pawnbrokering offers, whole segments of society would be cut off from sustainability.

Ironically, these pawnbrokers understood a good investment better than the more exclusive traditional bankers. Today collectors of fine artisanal pieces specifically look for "old pawn"—high value, heavier pieces generally from the 1920s and 1930s that were pawned and never redeemed. "Dead pawn" refers to both old and newer, less valuable pieces that have not been redeemed.[32]

---

30.   A desert transformed: Water reclamation key to growth, http://www.srpnet.com/about/history/water.aspx#top.

31.   Teresa J. Wilkins, *Patterns of Exchange: Navajo Weavers and Traders* (Norman, OK: University of Oklahoma Press, 2008).

32.   The Collector's Guide to Santa Fe and Taos—Volume 11, http://www.collectorsguide.com/fa/fa063.shtml.

Most fine jewelry and works of art from any genre are redeemed because of the inherent and personal value of the pieces. However, a small percentage of this high-end collateral is not, making pawnshops interesting grounds for intrepid bargain hunters.

SURVIVAL OF THE FITTEST

Pawnshops and their variants have been an integral part of society throughout history. In the early stages of human society, they existed as a simple, easy to understand cog in the economy. With the onset of glorifying ivory tower thinkers without questioning the reality of their theories, monetary policy became removed from simple transactions to survive to immoral activities. Religious and political leaders arbitrarily chose biblical passages and philosophical writings to set out rulings that suited their own struggle for control over people, equating brotherly support with socialistic dependency.

But no one—from workmen to bishops to warmongering kings—could deny the pressing need for cash flow. Religious leaders collaborated with lenders to develop complex red tape transactions to disguise usury as administrative and transactional fees to avoid the Jewish, Christian, and Islamic prohibitions on usury. In countries where pawn lending was officially sanctioned or where the frontier was wide open, the perceptions of pawnbrokers' services were back to where they were during the Bronze Age—simply part of daily survival.

Despite the continued efforts of social leaders to suppress and control access to cash and credit flow, necessity always prevailed even in the most oppressive regimes. And as usury unfettered itself from moral taint in industrialized countries, it became an accepted and expected part of doing business. However, this presents a new challenge to the pawnbroking industry. As the lending institutions of the middle and upper classes look for more profit opportunities, they have sought to demonize the ever straightforward pawn industry in favor of their whitewashed, steel tower Wall Street robber barons disguised as the liberal elite who "care" about the "exploitation" of the working class. On the one hand, these six and seven figure salaried financiers and their Washington, D.C., minions reach out to lift up the working class into the middle class status quo, even while the other hand is robbing the taxpayer piggy bank. And yet they unabashedly point their greased fingertips at the honest pawnbroker as no better than a loan shark.

Still, searching through the history of any subject outside the "mainstream" is a treasure hunt in and of itself. The history of the pawn industry isn't contained by the dusty underworld of dingy shops in ghetto neighborhoods. It isn't just a diatribe about the unfair ways pawnbrokers have been treated. It abounds with exotic treasures, entrepreneurial endeavors, celebrity, and mystery, and a little bit of self-satisfied "I told you so" as the bailout fiasco unfolds across America and impacts the worldwide economy.

CHAPTER FOUR

EXOTIC TREASURE AND IRRELEVANTLY FUN FACTS
Or Is This A Garage Sale?

The pawn industry, by dint of being lenders of last resort, has had unique opportunities to fund some interesting projects that traditional funding sources passed on as too risky. Another benefit of their bottom of the barrel status has been to take in some cool collateral from desperate kings, queens, and upper-class patrons whose bankers weren't about to lend them another dime. Who says fringe landing doesn't have fringe benefits?

BRING US AN IDEA, NOT A CREDIT SCORE

The pawn industry doesn't care about your credit score. Frankly they don't care about your ideas either, but they make for interesting stories when ideas come to fruition because of a transaction made by a pawnbroker. Entrepreneurs and inventors throughout history have relied on pawnbroking services to benefit a wide variety of industries. And if the idea's good, the pawnbroker is not the only one who benefits from the transaction. Sometimes, all of mankind does.

PRINTING

Johannes Gensfleisch zur Laden zum Gutenberg (c. 1398 – February 3, 1468), was the first European credited with inventing the mechanical printing press. He is famously known for printing the forty-two-line Gutenberg Bible. Less widely known, the entrepreneurial Gutenberg had pledged his printing press as collateral on a business loan from Johann Fust to pursue the Bible and other printing projects. The business quickly ran into debt, even with additional cash bailouts from Fust, and Gutenberg was unable to make loan payments. Accusations of embezzlement were made. The court, most likely disgusted with Gutenberg's expensive forays to deluxe resorts in balmy Mainz, Germany forced him to surrender his invention to Fust.

This just goes to show, borrowing money from your pawnbroker is far less risky than from your partner. The terms are much clearer, and the legal fees are less.

PHARMACEUTICALS

In China, an entrepreneurial scientist developed a new medication for diabetes. Needing about $40,000 to publicize the product and host a launch party (doctor conventions at tropical resorts are not cheap), he pawned his house to raise the cash (Ni 2001).

Given the price of prescriptions, that was hardly a risky investment on the part of the Chinese pawnbroker. In America risk is considered a cost of doing business for pharmaceutical companies, and protection is paid for in the form of high-priced attorneys, so-called expert witnesses, and Washington lobbyists. Just ask Merck, the makers of Vioxx.

Consumers would be better served if the FDA was run by the pawnbroker industry, or at least like it, since there is no marketability in dead human collateral.

COMPUTER TECHNOLOGY

In India, pawnshops are considered venture capitalists. The mechanical engineer who decided to branch out on his own and founded the Apara Enterprise Solutions, pawned "everything" he had (including jewelry and a motorbike) to raise the capital necessary to finance his venture in 1992. Today Apara is a leading provider of UNIX services to semiconductor firms in India.[33]

More industrialized countries have venture capitalists too. They're a little more formal though, requiring reams of marketing studies, business plans, and cost-benefit analyses. And you probably have to show up in a suit to beg for the money.

---

33.   Goswami, Amlanjyoti, Dalmia, Namita, Pradhan, Megha, *Entrepreneurship in India*, National Knowledge Commission, 2008.

Pawn brokers don't care what you show up in as long as the collateral is worth something. Unless of course you're pawning your suit.

CROWN JEWELS
extra! extra! isabella hawks the crown jewels for her lover!

Although rumors have circulated and certainly been perpetuated by Hollywood, there is actually very little likelihood that Queen Isabella II of Spain was Christopher Columbus's lover, and she did not actually pawn her crown jewels to finance his voyage. Not that she wasn't willing to though. Queen Isabella's quote inscribed on the statue "Columbus's Last Appeal to Queen Isabella," in the rotunda of the California State Capitol states "I will assume the undertaking for my Crown of Castile and am ready to pawn my jewels to defray the expense of it, if the funds in the treasury shall be found inadequate."

Columbus Before Isabella: Story of the Greatest Nations: Spain

She and her husband, King Ferdinand, were devout Catholics battling the Muslim Moors for control of the lands of Spain and Portugal. Since war, as we know all too well, is costly, Ferdinand had refused Columbus three times. But Isabella had visions of converting a whole new world to Christianity[34] and did indeed offer to pawn the royal jewels to do it. However, a friend and officer of the court, Louis Santangel, a convert to Catholicism, offered to advance Columbus the 2500 crowns necessary to equip three ships for his adventure.[35]

Now, there could be a story there between Santangel and the queen, but no one's telling. Then again, who would dare spread rumors with even a hint of truth about the queen who personally supervised the gruesome Spanish Inquisition?

A MELTING POT OF ALL THAT GLITTERS
the upper crust

The fancier pawnshops, especially ones with debonair clerks and owners with clipped British accents have the pleasure of taking in some glittery booty. It helps that they have the funds to finance the foibles of the international rich and famous. A Russian bringing in a diamond ring can walk out of Suttons and Robertsons in London's Belgravia (which will lend up to one million pounds) with a $75,000 short-term loan. Jim Tannahill, director, recalls one client bringing in a diamond ring for a $50,000 loan, which was used to finance a bar-restaurant venture. He has seen beautiful Faberge diamond bracelet set with cabochon sapphires and a priceless 40+ carat pink diamond owned by a wealthy Arab. "It was something to behold," says Tannahill. "God alone knows how much it was worth. We lent 250,000. It was a big thing, 40–50 carats. We'll probably see it again, we get a lot of repeat business." (Brennan, 2008)

Discretion, a "no questions asked" policy, lack of extensive paperwork and credit reporting, and convenience clearly make the pawn industry far more indispensable than your "friendly" community banker.

DUMP THE MAN, PAWN THE RING

Sometimes, however, pawnbrokers have the unpleasant (if titillating) task of telling the missus that the diamonds she's been flashing at the country club are

---

34.   Ellis, Edward S., Horne, Charles F., Story of the Greatest Nations: Spain, copyright 1901 by F.R. Niglutsch.

35.   Hunter, Thomas, *A Narrative History of the United States: For the Use of Schools*, American Book Co., 1896. .

really fakes. Tannahill elaborates, 'It could be that you come in ready to pay the school fees, and leave determined to seek a divorce.' (Brennan, 2008) Of course that's only if love is measured in carats.

Sometimes it's measured in square feet. One Chinese pawnbroker had a client who opened a piano bar in Shanghai. When business turned sour and he had a $100,000 debt looming, he needed to raise the cash fast. The only way to pay it back was to pawn the luxury apartment he had bought his wife as a birthday present. Since he was presumably alive to tell the story, one can assume he re-paid the loan, and his wife was never made homeless (Ni 2001).

OR MAYBE PAWN THE RING TO KEEP THE MAN

Miltons, Liverpool's premiere pawnbroking establishment, caters to the rich and famous too, who are quite astute at using current assets to develop long-term wise investments with sure returns. One of their clients, "a leading light on the Cheshire footballers' wives circuit—admitted that she was funding breast enlargement surgery by hocking her jewels" (Brennan 2008). Certainly she was counting on filling a large display area with bigger and better pendants, so it was clearly a sound investment with large returns in both interest and principle.

On this side of the Atlantic, Beverly Loan in Beverly Hills, California, is one of the few pawnbrokers in the country that makes loans of more than $10,000, catering to the rich and famous. They can boast of partaking in a modern-day Romeo and Juliet story, having lent $369,000 to Egyptian King Farouk's sister, who followed her heart by marrying a commoner and was disowned and short of cash.[36]

FOOD

Seriously, now, which would you rather have? A banker who gave you a free toaster or a pawnbroker who would be willing to give you a cash loan on food? (Actually, you'd be lucky to find a bank giving out lollipops in these days of cost cutting, but that's another story.)

---

36.   Calvin Sims, "A Pawnshop to the Rich: Business Is Picking Up," *The New York Times*, October 26, 1992.

If you happen to be a strapped-for-cash Parmigiano cheese manufacturer in Italy, you'd be in luck. The banks there take Parmigiano cheese in pawn for loans to the producers, storing the valuable cheeses in bank-provided vaults. If the loans are not repaid, the bank takes possession of the cheesy collateral. Not a bad deal, considering you can always shave a little profit off the top (Martinelli).

Belief in the marketability of purely American Coca Cola led one Florida banker in 1920 to enter a creative pawn extension to traditional crop loans for local farmers. He'd talk the borrowing farms into borrowing an extra $500 to buy Coca-Cola stock, and then use it as collateral in case the crops were poor and they couldn't repay the loan.

It was a win-win situation. If the farmers redeemed the stock, or if the banker kept it as collateral, one $40 share of stock in 1920 would now be worth millions because of company growth and many stock splits.[37]

The positive outcome of most pawn loans is perhaps never quite as tasty as those where food is used as collateral. As one pawnbroker put it, "a Virginia Country Cured Ham was pawned [and] at the end of 60 days it was not picked up so my employees and I enjoyed a very good lunch."[38]

THE STRANGE AND MYSTERIOUS

Food and baubles aside, pawnbrokers have seen items worthy of X-file entry as collateral. Hardly the most esoteric examples, but worthy of honorable mention are the Lamborghini sports cars and a foot-long seventeenth century ornamental ivory phallus Hatton Garden Pawnbroker in London's famous jewelry street has given loans on (Brennan 2008).

THE CRYSTAL SKULLS

Anyone familiar with the latest Indiana Jones flick has heard of the crystal skulls. Few may realize that they actually exist, but pawnshop historians and archaeologists know it to be fact, though no one knows for sure who made them. Polished out of a single crystal of quartz rock, they are mysteriously eerie. It is impossible

---

37. http://www.nextexit.com/dap/woc/hearth.html
38. Pawn Humor, FLA. PAWNBROKER, Summer 1995, at 33, 33

to even make an educated guess as to how long ago a skull shape was carved or polished out of the quartz. Two of the most famous clear crystal skulls are the "Mitchell-Hedges" skull and the skull at the Museum of Mankind (part of the British Museum near Piccadilly Circus in London). The museum reportedly obtained the skull from Tiffany's, the New York jewelers, supposedly part of an equally mysterious collection belonging to a soldier of fortune in Mexico.

The provenance of the Mitchell-Hedges skull is even more questionable since Mitchell-Hedges was a self-proclaimed British adventurer during the early twentieth century, notorious for a variety of tall tales. Although Mr. Hedges always claimed that he had found the skull in an ancient temple in British Honduras, there is a note from a British Museum staffer about him purchasing it at a Sotheby's sale from a Mr. Burney, an art dealer.

However, Hedges's adopted daughter, Anna Mitchell-Hedges, who inherited the skull when he died, explained her father pawned the skull with Burney as collateral for a loan. Weighing in at 11 pounds, 7 ounces and carved out of a single quartz crystal, her father often referred to it as the "Skull of Doom." He still rushed to redeem it when he heard that Burney was trying to sell it.[39]

A PRESIDENTIAL CAMPAIGN

Although nowadays you can apparently buy a Senate seat for the right price from the former governor of Illinois, it usually costs a ton of money to run a winning political campaign. Just ask President Barack Obama. His campaign is still trying to sell stuff to pay off Hilary Clinton's debt. We doubt if he'll have to hock anything to do so (other than our future tax payments), but we know of at least one who did.

Lady Bird had told Lyndon Johnson, prior to marrying him, "I would hate for you to go into politics." But love overcame politics, at least in her case. She used her inheritance as collateral to obtain a loan to finance his campaign for US Congress, when he ran in a special election in 1937.[40] It turned out to be a wise investment many years later as her husband became President of the United States.

---

39.   Carmen Istrate, The Eerie Crystal Skulls, 2005-03-02.
40.   *Lady Bird Johnson*, womenshistory.about.com/od/1stladyjohnson/p/lady_bird.htm.

RELIGIOUS RELICS

Pawning priestly vestments and insignificant church accoutrements was as commonplace as the poor in England pawning their Sunday church suit on Monday and picking it up on Saturday. But pawning great religious artifacts certainly took some chutzpah. Maybe that's the true symbolic meaning of the famous pawnbroker logo of three gold balls.

In 1238, Latin Emperor Baldwin of Constantinople ran into great financial difficulty—typical of kings and emperors of the day as they financed their wars and colonial exploits. Being the leader of Byzantium as well, he decided to pawn the religious relics that he had access to with a Venetian broker, including the Crown of Thorns.[41] Rather than let the relics fall into private hands, Saint Louis, the king of France, took over and paid back the Venetians.

Unfortunately no one places as much value on artifacts like "life, liberty, and the pursuit of happiness," or "no taxation without representation." We Americans can hardly expect that anyone will come to our rescue and redeem these pawned ideals. We have become an eBay nation, where everything, it seems, is for sale to the highest bidder.

HUMAN COLLATERAL

Although we might all feel a little sheep-herded right now as our futures are being sold left and right in the venerable halls of our government in Washington D.C., in reality human beings have been used as collateral on loans and to repay debt throughout history and all over the world.

In response to the Chicago's "slavery disclosure ordinance," companies looking to bid on city contracts must hire historical researchers to pore through their history and the history of all companies they merged with and disclose any records of slave ownership and/or transactions that involved such ownership. Many companies have unfortunately discovered a lot of transactions that involved human collateral, and some owned slaves outright when borrowers defaulted on loans:

- Georgia Railroad and Banking Co. owned at least 162 slaves.

---

41. Ecclesiological Society, *The Ecclesiologist* (Cambridge: Cambridge Camden Society, 1855).

- Bank of Charleston accepted at least 529 slaves as collateral on mortgaged properties or loans, and subsequently acquired an undetermined number of slaves when customers defaulted on their loans.

- Wachovia admitted to slave ownership, but said "incomplete records made it impossible to know exactly how many slaves were owned by the predecessor banks."

- JPMorgan Chase & Co., seeking to finance a bond issue for Chicago in 2003, reported in January 2005 that two of its predecessor banks in Louisiana accepted slaves as collateral on a loan and later owned more than 1,250 slaves.[42]

Additional records exist for individual transactions where slaves were frequently used as collateral on loans. One such example shows how mortgaging human beings broke up entire families as if they were no more than separate stock options:

"Benjamin Brittain was listed as the owner of 11 slaves in 1830. Records show Brittain used the slaves frequently as collateral in loans. One, Esther, and her youngest child were finally lost when a business deal soured: 1828 Brittain mortgaged to Robert B. Vance estate Esther and children Boston, Will and Ransom(1) (Bk. A, 189, 224) 1835, Mortgaged to Vance estate: Esther's two youngest children, Sarah and Clarissa (Bk. A, 265)1838, Brittain & J.K. Gray mortgaged to Henry Grady and John Hall: Esther, abt. 35, and her child (Bk. B, 701)1838, Brittain mortgaged to Thos. J. Roane: Isam, Boston, Wilson, Ransom, Esther, Lawson, Dick, Jane, Sary, Clary (Bk. A, 573) 1838, Brittain mortgaged to Jesse Pendergrass, Geo. Carson and John Hall: Isham, Ned, Boston, Willson, Ransom, Susan, Marlborough, Easter, Jane, Sarah and Clarey (Bk. A, 616) 1839, Sheriff Eli McKee sold at courthouse in Franklin, to satisfy judgment against Benjamin S. Brittain, a Negro woman Esther, about 35, and her child Betsey, about six months, to N.W. Woodfin and Wm. H. Thomas, for $660."[43]

---

42. *Wachovia apologizes for historical ties to slavery; Georgia bank cited*, Atlanta Business Chronicle, Wednesday, June 1, 2005.

43. *Brittain Slave Records*, Olden Times in Macon County, NC & News of the History Scene Today, March 2000

In Africa, although slaves could be pawned, both borrowers and lenders apparently preferred to pawn their family rather than foreign slaves. In Asante culture, pawning was not considered in the same category as slavery as a form of exploitation. Pawns were recruited from the "free" subjects of the Asantehene, although all the pawns were poor (otherwise they could have redeemed themselves) and dependent on elders or masters. These masters used their dependents' labor to repay debts. It was only if a pawn's abusua (person they were dependent upon) fell into deeper debt that the pawned relative might find her or himself sold out of the family altogether, as a slave.[44]

In Europe and Britain, pawns were often royalty, not poor relatives. In 1485 the Earl of Richmond (later to become King Henry VII) used the Marquis of Dorset and Sir Thomas Boucher as collateral for a loan from the king of France. He later borrowed six thousand marks from the citizens of London and redeemed the royal pawns.[45] Medieval royalty often used their children as pawns in international dealings with other royal families. One famous example of this was when England's King Edward refused to allow his two younger brothers to marry the Neville girls, which would have put more power into the hands of his greatest rival.[46]

The more adventurous Europeans actually offered their own children as collateral to fund colonial exploration. One such sailor, Sebastian Vizcaino, a Basque soldier who had gained some fame fighting for the Spanish army's galleon in Flanders, was aboard the Santa Ana, when it was attacked by the infamous pirate Thomas Cavendish. He had spent some time involved with business in Mexico before boarding the Santa Ana with his goods.

Parlaying praise from the king of Spain for his valiant efforts during the pirate attack, as well as from the viceroy of Mexico, he sought to explore the riches of California, obtaining authority for a private expedition to seize and settle lands in northern California. Vizcaino also bought a license to fish for pearls

---

44. Gareth Austin, "Human Pawning in Asante, 1800–1950: Markets and Coercion, Gender and Cocoa." in *Pawnship in Africa: Perspectives on Debt Bondage.* Ed. Toyin Falola and Paul E. Lovejoy (Boulder: Westview Press, 1993), 119–159.

45. Harold Dambrot, *History of Pawnbroking,* Gem Pawnbrokers Corp.

46. Luan Gaines, from an interview with Sandra Worth, the author of *The Rose of York* trilogy, http://www.curledup.com/intworth.htm.

off California. Seeking financing for his expedition, Vizcaino offered to put his seven-year-old son in pawn for two thousand pesos.

Although he had some trouble with the new viceroy, who had grave misgivings that a Basque merchant and soldier, regardless of past exploits, would be able to represent the royal king in "so great an enterprise," Vizcaino's expedition proceeded in March of 1596, with "three ships, four Franciscan fathers to convert the natives, and a force of soldiers with some wives and horses."

His first expedition failed miserably, and when he returned to Mexico, he found is reputation had suffered. Ever the determined explorer, he spread propaganda of "pearls as plentiful as fish, of rich salt deposits, of natives begging for Christianity, wearing gold and silver ornaments and clad in cotton cloaks of luxury" in order to get the king to give him another chance. Somehow he not only convinced the new viceroy to authorize the second expedition, but he actually obtained partial financing from the Crown.

On this second expedition, Vizcaino, who offered his son up as pawn collateral to finance his trips, discovered San Diego. In defiance of his specific orders limiting the scope of his trip to pearl hunting and proselytizing, he traveled with a mapmaker and renamed everything (his maps and names survive today).[47]

ART AND BOOKS

Artists and scholars are known to look down their collective snobby noses at plebian monetary matters. However, many have been forced by circumstance to recognize the monetary conversion value of books, manuscripts, and works of art and have made use of them as collateral for many loans that have kept them afloat.

Although universities and colleges were often the source of many scholarly works denouncing the practice of collecting interest on loaned money, apparently the lofty librarians understood all too well the value of collateralized lending. The Balliol Library of Oxford University in the medieval period had developed quite a collection of books, many left to the library in wills. By the first half of the fourteenth century a valuable collection had been acquired.

---

47.   Richard F. Pourade, *The History of San Diego*, San Diego Historical Society.

Beyond the essential scholarly purpose of these books, they also represented assets that could easily be pawned as collateral to the university if the college needed operating money quickly. The volumes, when not in use, were thus carefully stored for both their academic worth and the capital value to the school.[48]

Artists also recognized the less lofty need for food and shelter and often had to pawn their work for the cash for these necessities. Whistler's famous work *Mother* was pawned on numerous occasions when he fell on hard times. But by 1891 pride and perhaps as sense of long-term benefit to his reputation led Whistler to arrange for the French government to purchase it for the Luxembourg Museum in Paris. While he sold it for a mere four thousand francs, Whistler knew that most pieces in the Luxembourg would eventually find their way to the famous Louvre museum.[49]

Unfortunately, art has been collateralized for less honorable reasons than to feed a starving artist by banks not as used to checking for stolen goods as pawnbrokers are. The criminals know that the heavily regulated pawn industry is not a safe place to fence stolen goods. But art theft experts have advised leading banks around the world to check their vaults for stolen masterpiece paintings, which has become a growing crime. Figures released in 2008 by the Art Loss Register in London showed that 349 Picassos are missing worldwide, with five of his etchings stolen from a London gallery in June 2008.

The Art Loss Register currently lists missing art works worth over one billion pounds, including 250 works by the Russian artist Marc Chagall, 175 by Dali, 121 Rembrandts, 112 Renoirs, 269 by the Spanish artist Joan Miró, and 119 by pop artist Andy Warhol. Most, if not all, is believed to have been offered as collateral to banks to finance international crime, because most accept works of art as pawn for loans without checking their ownership. Only recently aware of the practice, banks have already encountered the following:

- In 2007, a £500,000 old master, discovered to have been stolen from a Milan gallery in 1993, was brought into a London bank for valuation to secure as a loan a year after being sold at Christie's in London.

48. Jones, John, *Balliol College, A History* (2nd ed.) Oxford: OUP, 1997
49. The Art Museum Junkie, http://wordpress.com/tag/the-art-museum-junkie/, October 12, 2008.

- Two paintings from the Beit collection, stolen from Sir Alfred and Lady Beit in the Irish Republic, are believed to have been used to obtain $1 million for Irish gangsters.

- Vermeer's *Lady Writing a Letter with Her Maid* and Goya's *Portrait of Dona Antonia Zarate* were later found in a Luxembourg bank after being handed to a Belgian diamond dealer in return for the money.

Of course art insurers are leading the efforts to make these leading banks do at least some of what any small pawnshop is required to do. The irony according to Scotland Yard, is that this extra work would actually benefit banks as well since they believe a lot of what is taken as collateral isn't even genuine.[50]

Perhaps Scotland Yard should take a second look, since bankers may even know this. Although they may try to put themselves on some lofty pedestal above the lowly pawnbroker, in fact they are primarily in business to do the same thing—loan money for interest. And if the payments are coming in, they aren't going to complain. With the way banks operate, their risks are much lower than that of a pawnbroker, so it may not be in their best interest to look too closely at the collateral.

Scotland Yard need only look across the Atlantic to see how eagerly bankers and mortgage brokers colluded with appraisers and realtors to convince buyers that houses were worth the prices that they happily lent millions of dollars of "bubble" money on. When the bubble burst, these lenders aren't sinking with the ship—they're being bailed out by Congress, which has been bought and paid for many times over as an insurance policy against this risk.

LAND, TAXES, AND JEWELS: ROYAL PAWN FOR LOVE AND WAR

Although mentioned in general terms before, it bears repeating that the elite around the world and throughout history have been and always are ready and willing to pawn what ought to be public property or treasures to fund both war and love.

---

50. Reid, Tim and Milner, Catherine, *Stolen Old Masters raise cash for crime*, The Sunday Telegraph London; December 7, 1997.

Kings and queens were not the only elite borrowers. The crusaders knew a thing or two about the value of location and design in real estate as well and parlayed that into ready cash for wars. The Cafarlet (or Capharlet) fortress, reconstructed from the earlier Arab fortress, was built along the biblical pilgrimage route from the north (Acre, Haifa, Atlit) to the south (Caesarea and further to Jerusalem). In 1213 the fortress was given to the order of "Hospitallers" (the order of the Knights of the Hospital of Saint John) as collateral on a loan. This valuable piece of real estate was later sold to the order of the Templars in 1232.[51]

This was not the only crusader fortress to have been used as pawn collateral. In the early 1400s the Teutonic Order lost its military supremacy as Europe realized that there weren't any pagans left to be converted. The Prussian cities no longer felt it necessary to pay the high taxes enacted to fund the upkeep of the Teutonic Knights. The knights futilely attempted to force the cities to pay high taxes, which led to the secession of the Prussian federation in the Prussian War (Thirteen Years' War) from 1454 to 1466.

In an attempt to beat the Prussian rebels, the Teutonic Order hired Bohemian soldiers (Hussites), and unable to pay the Bohemians, the knights handed them over the famous Teutonic fortress—the Marienburg (Malbork)—as collateral for the cost of the soldiers. As the order was unable to repay, the Bohemians sold the Marienburg to the Polish king.[52]

If fortresses in strategic locations were valuable collateral, whole cities and towns were even more so. In 1273 German King Rudolph of Habsburg took the town of Eger as the spoils of war from King Otakar of Bohemia. A short time later King Rudolph's daughter Judith got engaged to Wenzel, the son of King Otakar, and King Rudolph used the entire Eger area as collateral security on a dowry of ten thousand marks in silver.

In a bit of homage to the incestuous royal intermarrying of the time, Emperor Adolph von Nassau, King Rudolph's successor, renewed the imperial pawn status

51.   Ha-Bonim, http://www.biblewalks.com/Sites/HaBonim.html.
52.   C. Moeller, "Teutonic Order," in *The Catholic Encyclopedia* (New York: Robert Appleton Company, 1912).

of Eger in a bid to have his son Ruprecht marry now King Wenzel's daughter Judith.[53]

As a precursor to the ways in which the Federal Reserve operates in the United States, and much like what was orchestrated later in England by the Rothschilds (then called Fuggers), Scandinavian kings pawned the rights to future taxes and fees to finance present national debt. In the 1300s, the underage king of both Norway and Sweden, Magnus Eriksson, entered a series of expensive but failed wars; almost all rights to taxes and custom fees were given in pawn to the creditors of the realm (mainly the counts of Holstein).[54]

This loss didn't stop the Danish king in the last part of the fifteenth century (who now ruled Norway, Denmark, and Sweden) from pawning the two islands of Shetland and Orkney to Scotland as dowry for the marriage of his daughter Margaret to Prince James of Scotland, and in 1469, Shetland and Orkney were to be returned to the royal government of Norway when the debt was paid. When that never happened, Scotland obtained complete control over the islands.[55]

Sometimes the royals took land as collateral for private lenders. During the Dutch Revolution for independence from Spain in the 1500s, Queen Elizabeth I held the lands of Flushing and Rammekins as "collateral" before she would let the London merchants advance money or send soldiers to the Dutch.[56] She also secretly pawned one of the royal Crown Jewels, the over fifty-five carat famous Sancy diamond,[57] to finance the Dutch war against Spain.

This was not the only time a British royal pawned the Sancy diamond for war. In the 1600s, Queen Henrietta Maria, wife of King Charles I, pawned the Sancy diamond to help finance her husband's civil war against Hull. When Charles had

53.   J. G. Sommer (1847), "Kingdom of Bohemia," vol. 15, pp. 301–337, Translation Copyright 2001 by Urs Geiser.

54.   About Denmark, Part 3 of the soc.culture.nordic-FAQ, Lysator Academic Computer Society, Linköping University, Sweden, 1998, http://www.lysator.liu.se/nordic/textvers/part3.html.

55.   Lasse and Mads Age, "History of Shetland," http://home.no.net/fossh/ungdomtr/shetland.htm, 2002.

56.   William Elliot Griffis, *Belgium: The Land of Art—Its History, Legends, Industry, and Modern Expansion*, (Boston and New York: Houghton Mifflin Company).

57.   The Sancy diamond, currently at the Louvre Museum in France, has a long history of being bought, sold, lost, and pawned by royalty and wealthy families (including the Astor family), according to http://famousdiamonds.tripod.com/sancydiamond.html.

her leave to Holland out of concern for her safety, she took the British Crown Jewels to sell or pawn in order to raise monies and munitions should armed conflict break out between her husband and Parliament.[58] Never mind the fact that the Crown Jewels did not belong to her—it wouldn't be the first or last time that the governing elite used a country's treasure for their own purposes, or the purposes of their cohorts. In 2008 the U.S. president, the Treasury Department, and the Federal Reserve took action in the middle of the night to give AIG, a private insurance company, billions in U.S. taxpayer dollars to rescue them from bankruptcy, further guaranteeing the loans with future taxpayer money, with the interest on this money going to the private bankers that own the Federal Reserve. Although convoluted and using plenty of collateral, we can hardly call the Federal Reserve pawnbrokers, however. That's because their risk is nil, and the true lender is the American taxpayer—only the Federal Reserve gets to collect all the interest.

Perhaps they took a lesson in history from Napoleon, who was an expert at using other people's possessions as collateral and then had the nerve to collect the benefit of that collateral as well. In 1797 he took possession of the Regent, a 140-carat diamond, owned by Philippe d'Orleans who mysteriously "disappeared" during the French Revolution. Napoleon pawned it to fund a war and, when redeemed, mounted it in his own royal sword.[59]

Apparently, the American elites took far more valuable lessons in monetary policies than in principles of liberty represented by a French statue. If pawnbrokers stole on such a regular basis, they'd all be thrown in jail. Regulations that police the pawn industry are regularly and vigorously enforced, unlike the convoluted and ever-nuanced financial, banking, and corporate laws that never seem to quickly bring justice to white collar thieves. Oftentimes the wealthy perpetrators of these crimes never even see the inside of a courtroom, never mind a jail cell.

But it's all a matter of perception. Even if we are acutely aware of the unfairness in which blue collar lenders like pawnbrokers are treated in comparison to

---

58.   D. R. Watson, *Charles I*, (London: Weidenfeld and Nicolson & Book Club Associates, 1972).

59.   The Gems and History of France, http://www.goldsmith.it/us/culturale/storia/francia/francia.html.

white collar banks, brokers, and CEOs, there is so much propaganda out there clouding the truth we can't be sure what to believe.

Every day we are pummeled with news that is deliberately designed to frighten and separate us. Don't believe it? CNN had their chief business correspondent, Ali Velshi, roll out charts he created that showed that if we failed to back the bailout not only would these financial companies go under but the very companies we work for would as well. In other words, our ignorant opposition to being stolen from would cost us, our families, and our neighbors their jobs as credit markets closed and business would not be able to meet payroll.

All of this was farcical anyway, since well-compensated lobbyists had already paid Congress to assure that they would vote for the bailout regardless of what we wanted, but the dog-and-pony show had to be trotted out to ensure that voters would not revolt en masse against these same officials on Election Day. After that passes, we are told that if we don't support similar bailouts for private auto industries, we will be responsible for massive layoffs—regardless of the fact that these companies shipped more than those projected job losses overseas long ago. Again Mr. Velshi is put out front to explain to us ignorant plebeians why we should feel appropriately guilty if we don't support yet another white collar bailout.

Who is Ali Velshi, anyway? Is he some business or financial guru with multiple graduate degrees in economics for Harvard Business School or Princeton or Warburton? Well, not exactly. According to CNN's Web site's page on their venerated chief business correspondent (http://www.cnn.com/CNN/anchors_reporters/velshi.ali.html), he was "born in Kenya and raised in Toronto" and "graduated from Queens University in Canada with a degree in religion." He does have the valuable work experience of having been featured on the *Oprah Winfrey Show* and in "1996 was awarded a fellowship to the U.S. Congress by the American Political Sciences Association, and worked with now-retired U.S. Rep. Lee Hamilton, (D-Ind.)."

Well, that should explain everything. Mr. Velshi, educated in a combination of religion, politics, and media public relations, is actually the perfect person to explain the economic soundness of what the elites want us to do.

Never mind that dozens of the most respected economists in the country testi-fied that this was a horrid plan that would end up costing the future generations of Americans—our children—a chance at a decent standard of living. CNN, our *news leader*, put out the best propagandist money, experience, and education could buy to sell us our own poison and make us like it too. Yet again we are reminded that reality is spun by those at the top.

CHAPTER FIVE

USURY OR INTEREST
Or Is It Something Else That Stinks?

When we peel apart the layers of spin that colors our perceptions of various lending sources, we are able to see that all lenders charge interest, but not all lenders are equally fair. Even though the formal definition of usury is the act of charging interest, the reality is that the perception is different. Usury is perceived as "unjust" interest; even within the Catholic Church there has historically existed a conceptual difference.

But if we accept that all lenders collect interest as high as the market will bear, then it doesn't matter what we call it except from a public relations perspective. So is there anything else to be justifiably concerned about with lenders? Yes, there is.

From a fairness point of view, in the modern monetary system, there are two types of loans—those where the lender shares the risk and rewards of the transaction with the borrower, and those where the risk is deflected to some third party and the borrower, while the lender collects all (or an inordinate share, considering the lack of risk, of) the rewards.

Let's explore this core difference—whether by moral or religious argument—of the "risk" factor. Is the lender actively at risk of loss by the loan? If so, the lender should rightly be compensated for assuming that risk. In other words, there is a sense of fairness in the transaction. Many view investing money and expecting it to be returned regardless of the success of the venture being financed as a scheme for making money simply by having money (as opposed to doing so by taking a risk, engaging in some work or effort, adding value, or by sacrificing in some manner).

By this argument, it would seem that pawnbroker lending is innately fair. We have already established that the pawnbroker lends money without any collection of interest or even principle on the loan guaranteed by anything more than collateral given up front. If the loan is never redeemed, the pawnbroker has not collected any interest or fees up front and may never recover them at all.

Let us assume a $500 loan on a piece of jewelry valued at $1000:

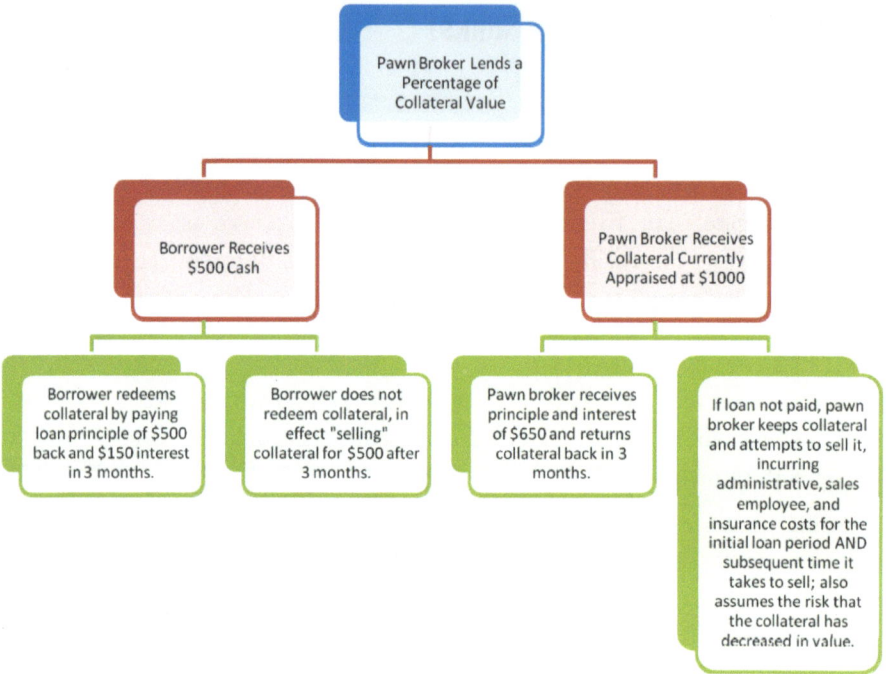

So the pawnbroker has shared the risk with the borrower, especially if the collateral loses value while in pawn.

CREDIT CARDS

Credit cards are adept users of slick public relations. They actively recruit their customers with alluring introductory interest rates in super-size letters and numbers, skillfully hiding the hidden fees and arbitrary hikes in interest rates in small print that can barely even be read let alone understood. They paint themselves as representative of the middle and upper classes, even cutting distinctions amongst each other. The intrepid Griffin family of the irreverent *Family Guy* show demonstrates this most in bitingly accurate humor when they refuse to take the Discover card at their new restaurant. As Lois Griffin puts it, the Discover card user belongs to an "exclusive club called everybody." Capital One, which behaves like a loan shark when a payment is even one day late, nevertheless tempts new consumers by offering the ultimate luxury of customizing your card. And of course American Express, belonging to the class of rich and famous credit card users, advertises with only the toniest actors and actresses to lure customers to their exclusive "club."

A recent study at Harvard University confirms the class aspect of different types of usury, calling credit cards the "mark of the middle class" (Littwin 2007). They are a status symbol, whereas pawnshops and other lenders have primarily low-income customers. Not only are low-income people enticed by the perceived class status of obtaining a credit card, they are further lured with the amount of credit offered and the minimum-payment option, which allows consumers to borrow more than through a pawnshop.

Credit cards offer an initial short-term lure of an immediate access to a large amount of credit at a relatively low cost, as opposed to a small amount of credit based on giving up a personal piece of collateral with a pawnshop, and it also acts as a temptation to spend more. Ironically, the perception that credit cards must be less exploitative form of lending because the middle class, which often has other financial borrowing options than the lower class, uses them is quickly turned on its head once the low-income users get trapped in a spiral of late payment fees and increased interest rates.

The study showed that as credit cards became more widely available and used by lower-income people the perception of them became increasingly negative. Failure to pay on credit card loans resulted in the long-lasting stigma of negative credit reporting and high costs attached to nonpayment. Missed payments were a never ending cycle of greater and greater debt burden.

If we compare pawn loans to credit cards, the inequities and truly abusive lending practices of the credit card industry become apparent. Unfortunately, because of slick advertising and the mighty stick of class appeal, most consumers don't discover this reality until they are caught in the net of spiraling credit card debt. Let's look at a simple comparison chart:

Credit Cards	Pawn Broker
• Minimum payment system obscures the full repayment costs of the loan. • Interest rate changes with a late payment or an over-limit fee, and additional fees are added as well. • Late payments on one credit card allows *other* credit card companies to raise your interest rate. • Available credit and interest rates is dependent on your credit score, which is a complex and ever-changing "collateral". • "Once you get it, it's way over your head." [Litwin, 2007] • "The advantage is that you can go out and get things that you do really need, that's without the wait. The disadvantage is paying back, like you're paying back at least twice. And you don't realize it because you're so happy that you got what it was that you needed or whatever it is. But in the long run it hurts. It truly hurts." [Litwin, 2007] • "[With loan sharks] you know what the situation is before you get into it.... But with the credit card companies, they're going to drain you slowly and take everything away from you. With the loan sharks, they might beat you up or whatever, but they're not going to come and take your house or your car or whatever is yours. They're not going to put you out on the streets. That's why I said I would much rather deal with them." [Litwin, 2007]	• The full cost of the loan is known and understood immediately, since the borrower must surrender control of the collateral up front in order to get the loan. • Terms of transaction are completely transparent and easily understood; they do not change in the middle of the agreement. • The sole consequence to not redeeming the collateral on time is loss of the collateral. • A credit score is not needed to obtain nor affected by a pawn broker loan. • Limited to those who have something of value to put up as collateral. • Loans are generally small and easier for low income users to manage. • "They're pretty useful I think because you can either leave it or get it back. And they don't charge much. You don't get much. So you don't have to worry." [Litwin, 2007]

Is there any wonder that this same study found that low-income consumers have a much more negative perception of this so called "middle class" status marker once they actually use credit cards?

Let's calculate the true cost of a $500 loan, both by a pawnbroker and by a credit card company[60]:

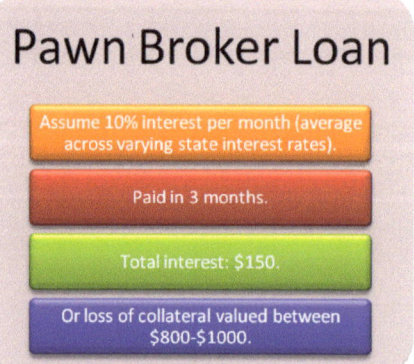

---

60. Using calculator on Bankrate.com for all credit card calculations.

Unfortunately what we can clearly see here is not nearly so clear to millions of misled consumers. And you can be sure that plenty of politicians and other false "advocates of the poor" are only too eager to try to extend out a pawn loan interest rate into some spurious 120 percent or greater APR. The fact is, this is purely misleading.

A pawn loan is not the same as a credit card or bank loan in that it is never meant to be a long-term product. An easier and better way to understand the ridiculous and misleading comparison is to compare a hotel nightly rate to a yearly rental. No one thinks of a hotel rate as dastardly—because it is understood that it is a short-term rental with greater risks associated with it for the owner of the property.

Further, no one would think it a valid comparison to put it into an annualized form. There has never been a politician or advocate out there claiming that at $100 a night hotels are exploiting poor consumers by charging them $36,500 in annual rent. Can you imagine the uproar of protest if someone dared make such a squalid comparison? Everyone but the most gullible would find it so ridiculous that the charge would be automatically dismissed and the claimant chastised for slanderous behavior.

Why are comparisons between bank and credit card loans and pawn loans allowed to continue then? Because very few people challenge propaganda spoonfed to us by sources we should be allowed to trust. It takes an enormous amount of energy to question the motives behind everything you see, hear, and read—especially since we are not in the habit of doing so. Questioning authority used to be every American's birthright. Now it's considered unpatriotic at worst and fringe politics at best.

And you can be sure that as long as it goes unchallenged these lenders will continue to make use of this PR because it not only makes their competition look bad, it also diverts attention from their own exploitative and deceptive practices.

These practices become even more apparent when a consumer is most vulnerable. As often happens with someone on limited income, one sickness or unexpected event can set a monthly budget awry. A day late on a credit card payment can dramatically increase the interest rate. Let's look at a scenario of two late payments:

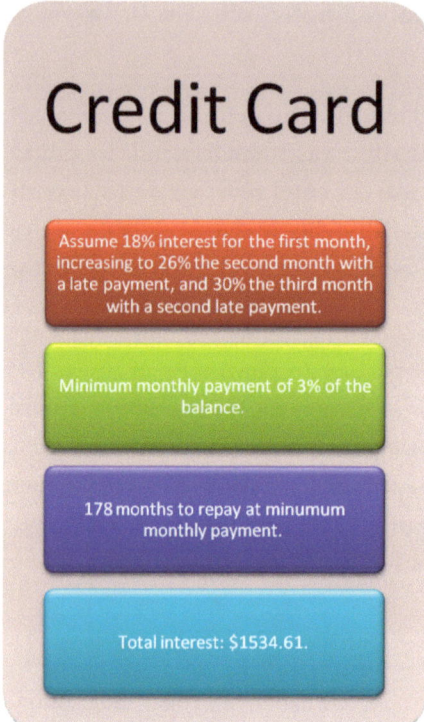

Credit Card

Assume 18% interest for the first month, increasing to 26% the second month with a late payment, and 30% the third month with a second late payment.

Minimum monthly payment of 3% of the balance.

178 months to repay at minumum monthly payment.

Total interest: $1534.61.

Pawn Broker Loan

Assume 10% interest per month (average across varying state interest rates).

Paid in 3 months.

Total interest: $150.

Or loss of collateral valued between $800-$1000.

BANKS: STATUS SYMBOLS AND PARAGONS OF VIRTUE

The general public needs to borrow small sums of money that other sources are not willing to provide, and this resulted in the rise in popularity of pawnshops. What chance do you think you would have of securing a $300.00 or smaller loan from a financial institution for a thirty to ninety day period? The cost of the paper work alone prohibits them from making such loans on a regular basis. Pawnbrokers offer access to these types of small loans, and inherent in the interest they charge is the cost of creating and maintaining the paperwork on the transaction, securing the collateral, and the cost of selling that collateral if not redeemed. In addition, pawnbrokers offer discreet access to cash for business owners who do not want their bankers to know they are having a temporary cash flow problem.

If we revisit the idea that sharing risk is indicative of a fair business transaction, we can clearly demonstrate that banks often do *not* act in fairness and, in fact, act "usuriously." Shockingly, even that most respectable of a loan, a bank mortgage, is in fact innately unfair. Let us revisit our pawn loan model, but instead of a $500 loan on a piece of jewelry currently appraised at $1000, we will use a $90,000 mortgage on a home sold for $100,000 with a 10 percent down payment from the buyer.

If the buyer defaults on the loan after fifteen years, the bank is in a positive cash position even if they sell the house for less than the borrower originally bought it for (not that far-fetched in today's housing market). The bank has incurred no costs *during* the period the borrower is not in default, since the loan requires that the homeowner maintain and secure the collateral. In addition, since the bank has collected its interest *first* and *every month* during the course of the loan, when the bank sells the house in foreclosure whatever it brings will go *first* to the principle loan balance.

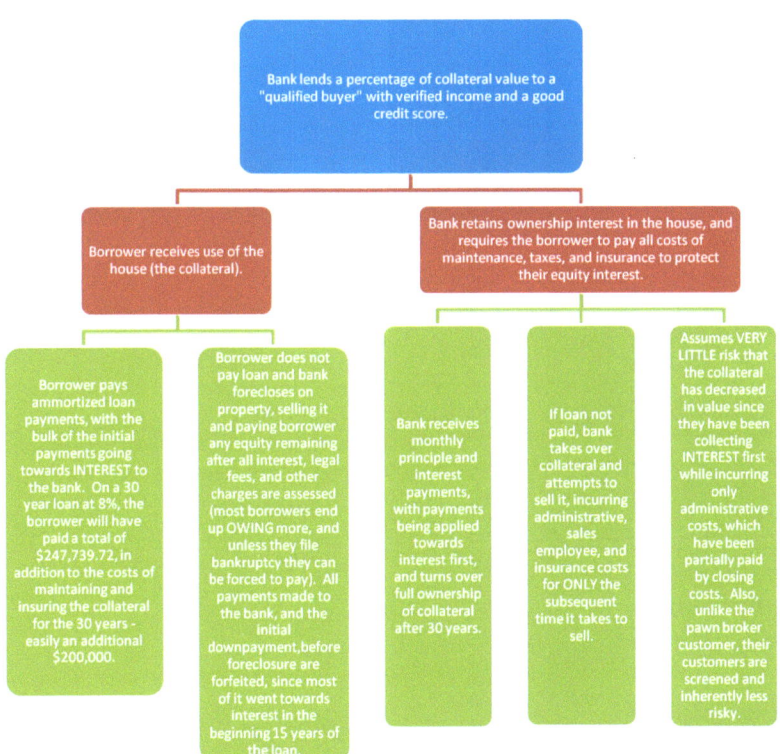

Let's look at what happens if a borrower who has paid for fifteen years on this loan suddenly defaults, and the bank is able to sell the house for $150,000:

	BORROWER	BANK
INTEREST OVER 15 YEARS	-$97, 974.00	$97, 974.00
PRINCIPLE PAID AFTER 15 YEARS	-$20,897.00	$20,897.00
PAID TO SELLER OF HOUSE	-$10,000.00	-$90,000.00
COSTS OF MAINTAINING HOUSE FOR 15 YEARS AT AN AVERAGE OF $1200/YEAR	-$18,000.00	0
COSTS OF INSURING HOME FOR 15 YEARS AT AN AVERAGE OF $1000/YEAR	-$15,000.00	0
EQUITY POSITION IN HOUSE IF HOUSE SOLD FOR $150,000.00 AT TIME OF DEFAULT	$80,897.00	$69,103.00
ADMINISTRATIVE COSTS OF FORECLOSURE	-$10,000.00	0
BALANCE, NOT COUNTING OPPORTUNITY COST TO LENDER OR RENTAL COST TO BORROWER	-$81,974.00	$97,974.00

Now let's look at the same scenario with the house selling at foreclosure for less than it was originally sold for:

	BORROWER	BANK
INTEREST OVER 15 YEARS	-$97, 974.00	$97, 974.00
PRINCIPLE PAID AFTER 15 YEARS	-$20,897.00	$20,897.00
PAID TO SELLER OF HOUSE	-$10,000.00	-$90,000.00
COSTS OF MAINTAINING HOUSE FOR 15 YEARS AT AN AVERAGE OF $1200/YEAR	-$18,000.00	0
COSTS OF INSURING HOME FOR 15 YEARS AT AN AVERAGE OF $1000/YEAR	-$15,000.00	0
EQUITY POSITION IN HOUSE IF HOUSE SOLD FOR $75,000.00 AT TIME OF DEFAULT	$5,897.00	$69,103.00
ADMINISTRATIVE COSTS OF FORECLOSURE	-$10,000.00	0
BALANCE, NOT COUNTING OPPORTUNITY COST TO LENDER OR RENTAL COST TO BORROWER	-$165,974.00	$97,974.00

In both scenarios the bank is in a positive cash flow position. By contrast, the pawnshop broker has *not* collected the interest up front and has assumed all the risk of securing and maintaining the collateral from the outset of the loan.

If the borrower does not redeem the collateral by paying back the loan and the interest owed, the pawnbroker keeps and sells the collateral. There is no other recourse against the borrower; in fact, the pawnshop sees this as if they "bought" the collateral. Many pawnbrokers encourage borrowers to sell the collateral up front if they have no intention of redeeming it by offering a higher sale versus loan price.

OVERDRAFT FEES

Another way that banks disguise the high fees that they would describe as "usurious" of pawnbrokers is through the "service" forced upon customers called an "overdraft fee." In a time when most retailers can and do electronically verify funds available on a paper check (or a debit card charge), a customer should be made aware immediately if they don't have enough money to cover a purchase. But of course this would mean that the bank would be giving the customer the option to *not* make the purchase, while they have every incentive to advance a loan they can charge exorbitant fees for. Regardless of the amount of the overdraft, a bank can charge a flat fee that can amount to interest rates that would make a pawnbroker blush.

The most insidious part of this practice is that unlike with a pawnbroker loan or even a conventional loan, the customer is given no opportunity to make an informed decision. Banks can even decide to process the highest dollar amount transaction first, in a day, causing every subsequent transaction to generate an overdraft fee.

OTHER TYPES OF COLLATERALIZED LENDING

Interestingly, the liberal elite often vaunt other types of collateralized lending that are quite similar in nature to that of a pawnbroker, but without the infamous moniker. Perhaps it is because they exist in third-world countries where traditional banks have not decided to pursue the vast market of the lower-income class, unlike in industrialized countries. The official sanction of the United Nations also helps, as a favored opinion of liberal elite thinkers.

The reality is that these lenders are simply the only access to credit in very poor countries. Like pawnbrokers, they have broken down the barriers of class and status to offer opportunities that were heretofore unavailable to most. Apparently as long as it is practiced "over there" and "not here," it is not only an acceptable institution but a lauded one. Someone more cynical might believe that has more to do with the commercial interests that traditional institutions here have in bad mouthing their competition as they try to extend their market share into the lower-income classes—and not any real concern for their well-being.

MONTE DE PIEDAD

The state-run Mexican pawnshop mentioned earlier also offers small business owners the opportunity to obtain loans at lower interest rates than banks. The rate of interest is determined by the type of collateral posted (Rose 1997).

MEFL

The Micro Enterprise Financing Limited (MEFL) is a nonprofit organization dedicated to assisting in the development of micro enterprises in designated inner-city and other urban communities of Jamaica. Conditions for financing include the following:

- Form a group and identify a group name

- Open a group savings account at a BNSJ for the purpose of making loan payment and facilitating compulsory savings

- Provide business equipment and machines as collateral[61]

GRAMEEN BANK

Grameen Bank was created as a viable alternative to conventional banking for poorer borrowers deemed as "not creditworthy," [62] and 96 percent of loans are for poor women funding entrepreneurship in areas that utilize indigenous skills, like embroidery, weaving, basket making, goat and cow herding, and poultry farming. Founded in Bangladesh in 1976, it boldly proclaims that access to credit

---

61. Micro Enterprise Financing Limited http://www.mefljamaica.com
62. Grameen Bank, Social Futures Observatory October 2006 43.

is a fundamental human right, fashioned as "interventionary philanthropy." Requirements include the following:

- Setting up a savings account, promoting the idea of economic security while also serving as collateral if the loan is not repaid

- Adherence to the "Sixteen Decisions" lifestyle that seeks to inculcate responsible entrepreneurial behavior [63]

- Substituting honor as collateral, Grameen borrowers are required to form a "solidarity circle," groups of five who must guaranty the loans of the other circle members[64]

JN MICRO CREDIT COMPANY

Fully owned by the Jamaica National Building Society, this company offers high-interest, small-business loans with collateral to entrepreneurs who cannot qualify for traditional commercial loans. Borrowers can use common household items as collateral.[65]

CULTUREBANK

The CultureBank is an interesting African initiative started in 1997 that offers credit to borrowers who use cultural objects as collateral. The objects are preserved and displayed in the CultureBank museum collection, "increasing awareness of Dogon history and cultural heritage, promoting the conservation of cultural resources in the local community, and increasing social capital among participants."[66]

---

63. Internet Based Social Lending: Past, Present and Future October 2006 Professor Michael K Hulme, Collette Wright B.A. M.A. Social Futures Observatory October 2006.

64. Grameen Bank Homepage, "A Short History of Grameen Bank," http://grameen-info. org/bank/hist.html.

65. JN Micro Credit Disburses Millions of Dollars to Small Businesses, http://www.jnbs. com/jnbs.dti?page=news&id=112 (November 4, 2002).

66. Tara F. Deubel and Dr. Mamadou Baro, *Conserving Cultural Heritage with Microcredit: An Impact Assessment of the CultureBank in Fombori, Mali*, Bureau of Applied Research in Anthropology, University of Arizona, 12/15/2002.

INDONESIAN MICROCREDIT

Another product Indonesian Pegadaian pawn branches now offer is microcredit, where small entrepreneurs can borrow to start an enterprise or upgrade equipment. Security required is a certificate showing ownership of property, like a house or motor vehicle (Graham 2007).

PRESENT DAY TRENDS IN PAWN BROKING

Today pawnshops can be found worldwide. Although there have been non-profit pawnshops established, most pawnshops are operated on a for-profit basis. The trends reflect family-owned businesses that have expanded or been passed down to other family members or state-owned monopolies. Relative newcomers to the industry are publicly traded pawnshop companies, like Cash America International, with over 450 pawnshops in the United States alone. Cash America was the pioneer of the chain pawnshop concept, with operations in the United Kingdom and Sweden as well. Another company currently expanding in the United States is EZCorp, with approximately 250 shops in nine states, and Super Pawn was the first non-Mexican pawnshop licensed in Mexico (Oeltjen 1996).

Interest rates vary widely from state to state in the United States and also from country to country. Different countries have some unique features:

- In India, pawnbrokers can go door to door to solicit business.

- In China, the counters in the shops are built high off the floor to protect the pawnbroker.

- In Hong Kong, the symbol for a pawnshop is not the three golden balls but a "winged bat (signifying fortune) holding a coin (signifying benefits)."[67]

- The logo for Indonesian pawnshops is the scales of justice, as used in the British court system, and reflects Indonesia's British colonial history (Graham 2007).

---

67. PRLog, "San Diego Jewelry Buyers Publishes History of Pawn Shops," http://www.prlog.org/10127090-san-diego-jewelry-buyers-publishes-history-of-pawn-shops.html.

- Pawn customers in China can take three years to redeem property, and the maximum interest rate per year is 3 percent.[68]

- "Pawnshops in other countries tend to deal primarily in gold and jewelry. But in China, we've lived under a command economy for so long, we don't own a lot of expensive accessories. If a small business needs $10,000 fast, what do they do? The most valuable thing they have is real estate," said Yuan Jingzhi, secretary-general of the National Pawnshop Assn., based in Tianjin, southeast of Beijing (Ni 2001).

- The National Gem and Jewelry Authority of Sri Lanka (the regulatory body of the gem and jewelry trade) provides technical appraisal training for those engaged in the pawnbroking trade.[69]

- Peruvian sheep farmers and commercial producers of sheep and sheep products use this livestock as collateral for loans.[70]

As mentioned earlier, Communist China under Mao took control of all financial institutions. Pawnshops were targeted and closed as symbols of "class oppression," but as China has moved toward a free market economy, they were allowed to open again in 1987.

The growing Chinese economy uses pawnshops as funding sources for entrepreneurs, with flexible collateral requirements. Whereas banks often will not lend to small and medium-size business owners with little credit history or lack of strictly defined "appropriate" collateral, pawnshops will lend on anything from real estate to "abstract paintings you drew yourself" (Ni 2001). "They are a huge help to private businessmen like myself," said Jiang Hua, owner of a Shanghai printing shop who frequently pawns his diamond ring and Rolex watch to solve cash-flow problems. "All my friends who run small businesses use them" (Ni 2001).

---

68. http://www.absoluteatronomy.com
69. Dr. Shihaan M. Larif, "History of the Gem Trade in Sri Lanka," http://jewelry-blog.internetstones.com/sri-lanka-gemstones/history-of-the-gem-trade-in-sri-lanka (February 13, 2008).
70. Food and Agriculture Organization, *People and Animals: Traditional Livestock Keepers: Guardians of Domestic Animal Diversity*, Rome, Italy: FAO Inter-Departmental Working Group on Biological Diversity for Food and Agriculture, 2007).

THE ADVANTAGE OF CUSTOMER SERVICE

No matter what country or state, the common theme is customer service; pawn-shop customers around the world are simply *more comfortable* using a pawnshop for a short-term loan than a bank, regardless of class. There are myriad reasons for this:

- No paperwork. "Our main competitor is Bank Danamon which is offering a product called Danamon Simpan Pinjam (DSP) for the bottom end of the market," said operations manager Swasono Widodo. "But the paper-work and procedures take time ..." (Graham 2007) People can turn to pawnbrokers at a moment's notice to help get them through a tempo-rary crisis—unlike a bank. With all their rules and regulations, the human factor has gone missing. Most bank managers—the ones who supposedly have the street-level connection to their customers—are little more than glorified clerks. They do not have the power or the training to make an immediate lending decision, regardless of the collateral.

- No credit checks or other verification requirements. In cash econo-mies, like Mexico, it is almost impossible for a person to demonstrate the financial ability to repay a debt that banks require. Also, only one in five Mexicans has bank account because most Mexican banks require customers to deposit at least $500 to open one, and a bank account is required for a bank loan, effectively closing this lending avenue for 80 percent of the population (Rose 1997). And in credit economies like the United States, the arbitrary nature of credit card lending practices and credit reporting make it equally impossible for most people to escape the ultimate arm-twisting torture device—the inscrutable FICO score.

- No credit reporting. And even if there were, pawn customers wouldn't receive a negative mark for not repaying a loan, they would simply give up their collateral. Also, many customers simply do not want a short-term loan to appear in their debt-to-income ratio because of the negative ef-fects on their credit rating. Traditional credit line lenders can arbitrarily raise the interest rates on other loans if a person's credit score changes due to additional debt regardless of ability to repay. This Machiavellian system is completely avoided by using a pawnbroker.

- Terms are clear and up front with no hidden fees. Unlike credit cards and even mortgage or personal loans, with the ways they collect amortized interest up front and can raise interest rates unilaterally, a pawnbroker transaction is easily understood. In fact, even if the collateral is not redeemed, the pawnbroker's retention of the collateral is not properly called a consequence, since it is not a punishment but simply a transaction fee. "Today, people in Italy use this bank service as a substitute for credit cards. Credit cards were introduced only recently in Italy, and the 18–25% interest on charges not paid off immediately, are substantial compared to the small fees charged by pawn-brokers" (Martinelli).

- Fast service. "Our system is different—it's friendly and fast—we strive to ensure that you can be in and out with money in your purse within 15 minutes. We're also open on Saturdays and in some places like Manado we operate at night. You don't have to open an account. The banks can't possibly match us" (Graham 2007). "The entire transaction—from request to payout—could take as little as 20 minutes."[71] "In the time it takes to process an application for a small loan from a formal lending institution, which may extend to months, a short-term loan from Monte de Piedad could be funded and repaid three times over" (Rose 1997).

- Discretion. As a Nashville lender said, "when they need extra cash—it may be for just a week or a month or two months—but the last guy they want to have know is their banker. They don't want him frightened" (Oeltjen 1996). In China, many shops still have discreet entrances in the back of the building for those who don't want to be seen entering a pawnshop (Ni 2001). Then there's the wealthy society matron in Philadelphia, Pennsylvania, "who pulls up in a chauffeured Rolls Royce every year at tax time for a loan against her baubles until her mutual-fund check" arrives (Polaneczky 2005).

It's ironic that the "lowly" pawnbroker offers genuine upper-class service. From the simplicity and ease of the transaction to the accommodations made to ensure the discretion of transaction, the pawnbroker industry truly offers the best

---

71. Working a Loan, Karl Eller Center for the Study of the Private Market Economy, Eller College of Business and Public Administration, The University of Arizona, Tucson, AZ, Fall 2000.

money you can borrow. There's no paper trail that exists outside the closely guarded shop records and no effect on the omnipresent FICO score, and it's a deal you know from the outset you can simply walk away from without any unknown consequences.

"IT'S THE ECONOMY, STUPID"

When the economy heads south and access to noncollateralized credit freezes up, the pawn industry finds itself in a position of growth and is a real opportunity for savvy investors. The U.S. economy both reflects and affects the global economy. Director Widodo of Indonesia's state-run Pegadaian

Unlike the U.S. banking sector, however, Indonesia's pawn shops report that nonperforming loans average about 5%. (Graham, 2007)

pawnshop company reported that it posted a Rp 500 billion (US $55 million) profit in 2006, with an almost 40 percent growth rate since 2005 (Graham 2007).

Reports from pawnshop executives and owners outline similar trends, regardless of the actual year of downturn:

- More expensive, "big ticket" items are pawned.

- Thus the individual loan amounts are higher.

- Customers look to stretch their purchasing power.

Alert owners limit lending on certain items, according to market conditions. For example, when the construction industry slows down significantly, they limit or stop taking tools in as collateral. Some pawnshops can now handle large, expensive items like cars, helicopters, and cranes.[72]

There are even companies offering collateralized loans as an alternative to venture capital loans in the burgeoning green energy field. Ethos Green Energy Asset Finance, LLC offers loans that are typically more expensive than traditional commercial loans, but far cheaper than venture capital loans. Ethos

---

72. Adam H. Beasley, "Pawn Shops Becoming the Banks of Last Resort," *The Miami Herald*, October 27, 2008.

cleverly turns the current economy and market conditions to its favor, advertising: "What if your investments could help solve America's addiction to oil, clean up the environment, and create outstanding returns? Ethos Green Energy Asset Finance, LLC (Ethos) strives to create high yield returns for our investors by extending asset collateralized loans to companies engaged in solving the most important challenge of our time."[73]

As in the past, today there's a predictable increase in the middle and affluent class using the accoutrements of status as collateral to fund everything from everyday living expenses to new luxuries:

- At Liverpool, England's premiere pawnbroking establishment, Miltons, the owners report a "smartly dressed and obviously professional" woman discreetly pawning a flawless pear-shaped diamond engagement ring, confiding that she needed "3,000 to pay the school fees." "The lady came in six weeks ago, requesting a small amount to pay the school fees," says Haywood Milton, director of Miltons. "She wanted a discreet, personal service" (Brennan 2008).

- Another Miltons customer recently pawned a piece of jewelry worth six figures to pay the thirty thousand deposit on a new Aston Martin. "He had a short-term cash flow problem," says Milton (Brennan 2008).

- Suttons and Robertsons in London, which will lend up to 1 million pounds, has seen a "huge rise in professional men and women bringing in diamond rings, watches, and other jewelry in return for quick cash."[74]

- At Carver Reed in Philadelphia, Pennsylvania, the owner recounts stories like the former football star who pawned a Super Bowl ring (which he never retrieved; it sold for $6,500), and the "weeping, laid-off CEO who knew he could borrow money against his wife's jewelry and not read about it in the Daily News' gossip pages the next day" (Polaneczky 2005).

---

73. Adam Boucher, President. Adam Capital Inc., http://www.adamcapitalinc.com/docs/ethos%20executive%20summary.pdf.
74. San Francisco Provident Loan Association, http://www.sfpla.com.

There are also companies (i.e., InstaCap) that help small "mom-and-pop" pawn-shops cater to businesses. They handle the logistics of securely storing large items, such as bulldozers and equipment for general contractors, and sufficient assets to make large loans, for a 5 percent commission fee.[75]

75. Working a Loan, Karl Eller Center for the Study of the Private Market Economy, Eller College of Business and Public Administration, The University of Arizona, Tucson, AZ, Fall 2000.

CONCLUSION

It's been my pleasure to assemble this glimpse into the pawnbroking industry for you. Socially, economically, and historically the industry has been filled with both colorful characters and stories. It still is. Over its thousands of years of existence, the industry has been controlled by governments, religious leaders, groups of elitists, and, most importantly, the requirements of the people the industry serves. Due to unreasonable regulation, religious beliefs, cultural predisposition, and economic conditions, the industry has been highly fragmented around the world. Yet it survives, and because of the current global credit crisis, the pawnbroking industry is experiencing a rate of growth greater than history has ever shown us.

As we crawl out of the ashes of the current financial crisis, traditional financial institutions (the ones who got us into this mess in the first place) will likely find a way to lobby and sway government regulators, just as they have always done. They will position and repackage themselves to be able to lure the lower-income masses into all-new high-interest schemes at low risk to themselves. Of course, they will appear as saviors because of their offer to serve the underserved, and because of their power and might, they will receive a legislative and economic advantage in the free market over anything allowable to the pawnbroking industry.

A pawnbroker, given free-market rein, can offer a fair loan based on collateral value and a finance charge that compensates him for the risk he assumes with a customer of uncertain income while charging a fee the market can bear. Overregulation of the industry, either greatly hampering or eliminating this free market, has proven time and again to harm the people who the industry serves by greatly limiting their access to credit.

As presented in this book, where they don't have the competition of traditional banks, the pawnbroker-like microlending institutions in third world countries are actually improving the image of high-interest credit companies by demonstrating on the world stage the benefits of offering credit access to low-income and presumably higher-risk groups. While these microlending institutions and the pawnbroking industry were never meant to be a substitute for mainstream consumer credit, you should now realize that short-term high-interest high-risk lending has always played a worthwhile part in fulfilling the needs of a credit hungry economy. More so now than ever, this group of high-risk lenders is providing liberal amounts of credit during a time when mainstream providers are busying themselves by slashing credit lines, adjusting interest rates, denying formerly qualified customers, and begging for further bailouts. Interestingly enough, many of these mainstream providers, even after realizing obscene amounts of profit, are still uncomfortable assuming any of the risk of their transactions.

I've been a pawnbroker for over thirty years. I cannot remember when risk has not been a part of my business and my life. I've always been the underdog, constantly battling an unearned dubious reputation, a falsely preconceived notion of my chosen career, an inaccurate and demeaning perception of the customers I serve, and a flood of unjust regulation coming at me from every angle. However, if I had it to do all over again, I wouldn't change a thing. Because even though I may or may not have convinced you of the unique worth and opportunities the pawn industry has and continues to represent in social economies, I'm reasonably confident I have shown you a wildly colorful fraternity of business people who are, in effect, the roots of modern banking and the oldest form of consumer credit. It does my heart good to know I am part of this fraternity. I am now and forever will be extremely proud to call myself a pawnbroker.

In this book, I have taken a few light shots at several institutions that are known to you. I did not do this with the intent of being malicious, disrespectful, or harmful in any way. I did this in hopes of expanding your perspective and understanding of certain beliefs that many of us were taught as children. Some of these beliefs that we have held as true since our childhood have recently been questioned, clouded, or trampled. While I do not hold a false hope of changing your viewpoint on these institutions, the current credit crisis, or the global economic conditions, I do hope I have at least entertained you and broadened your view of where the pawnbroking industry fits into the consumer credit market. I also hope I have been effective in explaining the "Pawnonomics" of the industry.

Conclusion

I occasionally wonder what the future of the pawnbroking industry will look like. Often called the world's second oldest profession, surprisingly little has changed in the industry over the past several centuries. But as I've shown you, the future direction of the industry is not in the hands of the people who are in it. This is nothing new for a pawnbroker, and we are a resilient bunch. As we emerge into a new economy, the future of the pawnbroking industry could be forever altered or even eliminated because of a number of different factors. But even if it were to be eliminated, I can guarantee you one thing. The need for the services the industry provides can never be replaced and will never be eliminated.

BIBLIOGRAPHY

Brennan, Z. (2008, July 23). *Never too posh to pawn: From diamonds to antiques - how the upper crust are coping with the credit crunch.* Retrieved from The Daily Mail: http://www.dailymail.co.uk/femail/article-1037343/Never-posh-pawn-From-diamonds-antiques--upper-crust-coping-credit-crunch.html.

Graham, D. (2007, February 5). Pawn Business in Indonesia: Freeing up the Loan Market. *The Jakarta Post.*

Hebrew Bible. (1917). Jewish Publication Society.

Littwin, A. K. (2007). *Comparing Credit Cards: An Empirical Examination of Borrowing Preferences Among Low-Income Consumers.* Harvard Law School. Cambridge: Harvard Law School Faculty Scholarship Series.

Martinelli, C. (n.d.). *The de' Medici Dynasty: The Late-Middle-Ages, Early Renaissance - Giovanni: The Founder.* Retrieved November 9, 2008, from Italophiles.com: http://italophiles.com/medici_2.htm#The_Early_Renaissance.

Ni, C.-C. (2001, March 26). Ad Hock Capitalism in China. *Los Angeles Times.*

Oeltjen, E. P. (1996). Florida Pawnbroking: An Industry in Transition. *Florida State University Law Review.*

Polaneczky, R. (2005, March 21). This Biz is a City Institution: Carver W. Reed & Co. Still Thriving After 145 Years. *Philadelphia Daily News.*

Rose, J. J. (1997). *MONTE DE PIEDAD: More than Household Finance.* Retrieved from Mexico Access: http://www.mexconnect.com/MEX/jrose/jjrpiedad.html.

The Holy Bible, New King James Version. (1982). Thomas Nelson, Inc.

ACKNOWLEDGMENTS

Thanks to my wife, Velma. She patiently listens to all of my pawnbroking tales with great interest and she finally convinced me to turn them into a book. Her love, trust, and faith rocks my world.

Thanks to my daughter, Amanda. Even when I'm far from at my best, her steadfast confidence in me always seems to put me back on the right track.

Thanks to Allyson Saad who burned the midnight oil doing the research for Pawnonomics. If you enjoyed this book and benefited from it in any way, Allyson gets most of the credit. If you did not, I will take all the blame.

Also, thanks to the pawnbroking industry for supporting my products at: http://www.pawnshopperformer.com/and http://www.pawnshopadvisor.com/ in my enduring attempt to leave this colorful industry in a better way than how I found it.

ABOUT THE AUTHOR

Steve Krupnik has been a pawnbroker for over thirty years. He founded the Indiana Pawnbrokers Association and is a past president. He is a former board member of the National Pawnbrokers Association and in addition to numerous governmental affairs awards; he was presented the Association's coveted "Pawnbroker of the Year" award in 1999. He currently resides with his family in South Bend Indiana and is a business coach and consultant to various industries, including the pawnbroking industry. His Internet blog on the pawnbroking industry is at www.pawnonomics.com